AVRELIO

AVG · LIB

APHRODISIO

PROC · AVG

A · RATIONIBVS

S · P · Q · L

DEDIC · Q · VARINIO · Q · F

MAEC · LAEVIANO · AED

INSCRIPTION FROM BASE OF STATUE IN A ROMAN PALACE
SET IN 'GOUDY OLD STYLE' CAPITALS

The Alphabet

AND ELEMENTS OF LETTERING

REVISED AND ENLARGED
WITH MANY FULL-PAGE PLATES AND OTHER
ILLUSTRATIONS DRAWN & ARRANGED
BY THE AUTHOR

FREDERIC W. GOUDY

L.H.D., LITT.D.

DOVER PUBLICATIONS, INC.

NEW YORK

Published in Canada by
General Publishing Company, Ltd.,
30 Lesmill Road, Don Mills, Toronto, Ontario.
Published in the United Kingdom by
Constable and Company, Ltd.,
10 Orange Street, London WC 2.

This Dover edition, first published in 1963, is an una-
bridged and unaltered republication of the work originally
published by the University of California Press in 1952.

International Standard Book Number: 0-486-20792-7
Library of Congress Catalog Card Number: 63-23603/CD

Manufactured in the United States of America
Dover Publications, Inc.
180 Varick Street
New York, N.Y. 10014

IN MEMORY OF

𝔅ertha 𝔐. 𝔊oudy

WIFE, FRIEND, COMPANION, AND CO-WORKER

WITH GRATEFUL RECOGNITION OF HER UNFAILING PATIENCE,

COUNSEL, AND INTELLIGENT CRAFTSMANSHIP

THIS VOLUME IS AFFECTIONATELY

DEDICATED BY THE

AUTHOR

PREFACE

WHEN 'The Alphabet' was first published it appealed mainly to persons, engaged in some form of the graphic arts, who needed more or less to use lettering in their work. Comparatively few readers at that time were interested in the cultural side of the matter, or cared greatly for the history of letters or their development. But since then there has come a decided awakening of interest on the part of the general reader, an improved taste both for the forms of the letters and for the manner in which they are used, and a more insistent demand for accurate information regarding the progress of letters from the clay tablets of ancient Assyria to Gutenberg's invention of movable types.

Since 'The Alphabet' has been out of print for some time, the author and publisher feel that an opportunity is offered for revision and for some additions to the text which will make a more comprehensive and valuable presentation of the subject than was contemplated in the earlier editions. With this idea in mind the author has added two chapters: one, which is here chapter i, to cover briefly the steps leading to the beginnings of letters themselves, and the other, chapter iv, to present the roman capitals, their origins and esthetic development, in greater detail than in previous editions. He has also added here and there new matter which he hopes will round out the entire subject more completely.

Four years after 'The Alphabet' first appeared, the author offered a companion volume, 'Elements of Lettering,' in which he presented plain letterings as models for students and included brief histories of each style shown. As the specimens given at the time of their making were developments of letters inspired by a study of the forms shown in 'The Alphabet,' it seems proper to

PREFACE

make 'Elements of Lettering' a part of the book to which it really belongs, so as to make it more valuable, and give the author an opportunity also to add matter at the proper places in the interest of greater lucidity.

As types and type design are now occupying the attention of readers in greater degree than ever before, the author, who for nearly forty years has endeavored by precept & example to arouse and foster a greater general esteem for fine printing and fine types, has dared to present some pages of a few of his later types, not as type specimens, but as examples of letters for a particular purpose, drawn & produced along the principles which are given herein.

The types in which this volume is set have been designed by the author.

F. W. G.

CONTENTS

CONTENTS

CONTENTS

et in conspectu agni amicti stolis albis et palme in manibus eorum · Et clamabit voce magna dicentes · Salus deo nostro : qui sedet super thronum et agno · Et omnes angeli stabant in circuitu throni et seniorum et quatuor animalium · et ceciderunt in conspectu throni in facies suas · et adorauerunt deum dicentes amen Benedictio et claritas et sapientia et gratiarum actio : honor et virtus et fortitudo deo nostro in secula seculorum amen Secundum Matheum

FROM A GERMAN MS. [CIRCA A.D. 1300]

The Alphabet
AND ELEMENTS OF LETTERING

INTRODUCTION

THE NUMBER of books dealing with lettering is now fairly large, some going more or less deeply into the history and development of letter forms while others principally present models or facsimiles of existing alphabets for suggestion or copying. The student-craftsman will do well to possess, and use, the volumes by Strange, Day, Brown, Johnston, and Stevens, together with the several portfolios of alphabets [Rhead, Smith, Johnston], as they contain matter not within the scope of this work.

Naturally, the author who attempts a contribution in a field already well cultivated should either offer new material or present in a novel and undeniably useful way what he has garnered here and there. For the present essay the writer claims no fresh discoveries in paleography; but he does wish to present his material in a distinctive and helpful form.

As to the text, he has taken his own wherever he has found it, and has incorporated the conclusions drawn from nearly forty years of work & study. He has not attempted to do more than outline briefly the results of his experience and explain the examples given ; nor has he endeavored to produce a handbook of paleography. He trusts, however, to find his account with the artist and craftsman who has real need in his work for letters that are legible and correctly drawn and that possess character and dignity as well as beauty.

[2]   Not all the letters shown here have been selected from the same sources; but where composite forms are given he has endeavored to bring them into exact harmony with the family into which they have been introduced. They serve also to trace the development of lettering, although there has been no intention of presenting the forms in exact chronological order. They indicate, further, how letters have been influenced by the tool used in producing them, and should suggest some of the endless variations which the craftsman may give without departing too far from traditional outlines.

Among the designs are free renderings of letters from sources not easily available to many who require to use lettering in their work. No attempt has been made to present quaint or peculiar forms, but rather to select the most legible and characteristic, those which will readily lend themselves to the needs of designers who wish to develop their lettering on a sound basis. The author has not always been able to find forms sufficiently legible or decorative, or easily adaptable to the student's use, and to meet the lack he has not hesitated to interpolate his own conception of the characters, reserving to himself, as it were, the same rights that the early artists exercised.

Some of the examples presented in collections of alphabets give the form of the letters but wholly lose the feeling that is an essential quality. In this work, therefore, special pains have been taken to convey that feeling & to preserve the delicate irregularities—practically lost in most reproductions—which contribute so appreciably to the character of the page in mass.* In type faces, it should

*A letter copied from one of Jenson's types by an artisan skilled in the use of bow pen, straightedge, & compasses might be an exact facsimile of that letter, but the

be understood that the spirit of the letter has been sought, rather than absolute fidelity to precise form, though the drawing, of course, has been done very carefully.

Most facsimiles of early manuscripts or of printed books are unsatisfactory because the reproductions are too small to exhibit the subtle variations clearly enough to enable the forms to be studied intelligently. The examples given here have therefore been drawn on a large scale, to insure easy analysis and comparison.

Typography and type design can only be touched upon in a manual of this kind, but the author feels that he may stress his aims in these matters for the reader's inference, since a book that is printed more or less under his care represents concretely the principles which guide him as typographer and type designer.

Good lettering must be founded on good models; for the use of beginners they ought especially to be simple, dignified forms that are free from the archaisms and mannerisms of the scribes and that exhibit in a high degree the essentials of legibility, beauty, & character. In the examples shown herein the writer has intended to provide typical letter forms only, showing old style, modern, and italic types, black-letter, stone-cut inscriptions, etc. He hopes that his selections will be found to answer every requirement.

The author wishes primarily to help the student-craftsman and, by precept and example, return the art of lettering to its original purity of intention—to bring a great craft again to life; it is not his aim merely to exploit his own achievements.

same letter drawn freehand by an artist trained to see the subtleties of line & form would possess a feeling & character that no mechanical construction can impart.

SENATVS POPVLVSQVE·ROMANVS DIVO·TITO·DIVI·VESPASIANI·F VESPASIANO·AVGVSTO

FIG. I   INSCRIPTION ON THE ARCH OF TITUS AT ROME. [CIRCA A.D. 72]

The Alphabet
AND ELEMENTS OF LETTERING

CHAPTER I : The Beginnings of the Alphabet*

F ALL THE achievements of the human mind, the birth of the alphabet is the most momentous. "Letters, like men, have now an ancestry, and the ancestry of words, as of men, is often a very noble possession, making them capable of great things": indeed, it has been said that the invention of writing is more important than all the victories ever won or constitutions devised by man. The history of writing is, in a way, the history of the human race, since in it are bound up, severally and together, the development of thought, of expression, of art, of intercommunication, and of mechanical invention.

* The author of *The Alphabet* advances no claim that in "The Beginnings of the Alphabet" he has presented any new facts. As his own particular line of study starts at the point where our roman letter forms came into existence, it seems desirable to touch briefly on the earlier history of those forms, accepting and using the conclusions of scholars, since he himself has neither the facilities nor the scholarship necessary to a successful study of Assyrian, Babylonian, or Egyptian picture writings and their development. The chapter is intended only to cover briefly the means of recording thought prior to the beginnings of Greek and Latin writing. The

[6]   When and to whom in the dim past the idea came that man's speech could be better represented by fewer symbols [to denote certain unvarying sounds] selected from the confused mass of picture ideographs, phonograms, and their like, which constituted the first methods of representing human speech, we have no certain means of knowing. But whatever the source, the development did come; and we must deal with it. To present briefly the early history of the alphabet requires that much collateral matter must be disregarded and a great deal that is omitted here must necessarily be taken for granted; the writer desires, however, to present what seems to him to be a logical and probable story of the alphabet's beginnings.

Although it has not yet been proved conclusively, it is quite possible, and altogether probable, that the traders of Phoenicia and the Aegean adopted both the use of papyrus and Egyptian hieratic writing, from which developed the Phoenician alphabet. Whether all the earliest writing systems of different countries sprang from one common stock of picture writing, we shall, perhaps, never surely know; we do know that the picture writing of Egypt exercised a very great influence, and it seems quite safe for us to assume that crude attempts by those ancient Nile-dwellers to express thought visibly or to record facts by a series of pictures—or by diagrams sufficiently pictorial, at least, to connect them with well-known objects [disregarding the earlier mnemonic stage or use of memory

author acknowledges here his indebtedness to the writings of Sir Edw. Maunde Thompson, Professor Petrie, Professor Breasted, Canon Taylor, Edward Clodd, Dr. Budge, Wm. A. Mason, and others for many suggestions. The chapter is merely his steppingstone by which he attempts to reach a point where his own field of study begins—the designing and use of letters themselves.

aids like the quipu or knotted cord, of which the rosary is a modern example]—constitute the origin of the abstract and arbitrary signs or symbols which we call "letters."

Let us assume, as logically we may, that picture writing in which a drawing depicting or suggesting the object itself came first; next must have come the ideograph, the sign suggesting the name of the object represented instead of representing the thing itself; & next the phonogram, or sign that suggests a sound only.

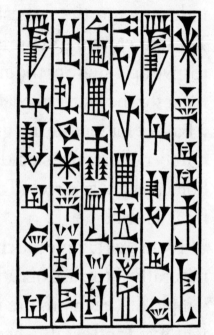

In the first class just named belong the wedge-shaped, or cuneiform, characters inscribed in the clay tablets, cylinders, and monuments of Assyria, Babylonia, & other Near Eastern countries—characters the very existence of which was overlooked or forgotten for some sixteen hundred years. They were almost purely pictorial—were

FIG. 2 CUNEIFORM WRITING ON A CHALDEAN CLAY BRICK

drawings only, really not writing at all, and, as far as we now know, have little direct bearing on the derivation of our present alphabet.

To this first class also belong the hieroglyphs of Egypt, highly elaborated types of picture writing which changed so little over a long period that "it is like a language which has never forgotten the derivation of its words, or corrupted their etymological forms, however much it may have altered its meaning." Developed at least five thousand years B.C., the purely pictorial character was preserved by its Egyptian users until the end. Sir Edw. Maunde Thompson asserts

[8] that "we may without exaggeration . . . carry back the invention of Egyptian writing to six or seven thousand years B.C." Most of the material available goes back not farther than the First Dynasty [3300 B.C.].

Possibly the earliest method of recording the payment of taxes indicates, too, the earliest stage in the process of learning to write. The farmer living on the banks of the Nile was obliged every season to give up a share of the grain or flax gathered from his fields as payment for the water needed to fill his irrigation ditches. A picture of a basket for measuring grain, together with strokes indicating the number of measures paid, rudely scratched on the mud walls of his home, served as a record of the payment and constituted his receipt for it as well.

From this simple parent of our alphabet a further step came quite naturally—the use of rude pictures to indicate other activities of a simple life, each picture representing an object the form of which was fixed and established and easily recognized as a sign to denote that particular object only and yet recall to mind some simple fact.

But this was not really writing: exact words were not represented; only simple ideas could be conveyed. Two steps had yet to be taken before the pictures would actually become phonetic writing. First, each object drawn had to attain a fixed form, easily recognized, always exactly the same and always denoting specifically the particular object depicted. The figure of the sun denoted that star only; a picture of a dog or lion, simply those animals. Later, when an attempt was made to express qualities as well, the pictures became figurative; thus the sun, in addition to its original sense, might denote glory, light, warmth; a lion, courage; the dog, fidelity; and so on. But even this symbolism was not adequate to encompass all the ideas incident to an improved civilization: a broader culture required a new picture and a new expression for each new idea, until finally the number became too great for easy execution. Then, too, there were many ideas too difficult to express by pictures alone, and hence requiring the invention or use of an arbitrary sign, called a "determinative," to be used with the picture, more definitely explaining its symbolism. A large number of the determinative signs that accompany many of the hieroglyphs on Egyptian monuments are graphic pictures of human or animal forms or their parts; they are descriptive of the words they depict and are always found after the sign which represents a word belonging to the category to which the sign itself belongs. To illustrate: a picture of an egg with a collection of signs indicating the name of a person would show that the person was of the feminine gender.

A picture of an object, no matter how crude its draftsmanship, sufficed to explain its meaning at a glance; but an abstract idea, as of virtue, love, time, sickness, space, required symbolism to make the meaning clear. The picture of a bee might indicate kinship or industry; a roll of papyrus, knowledge; a house, home or residence; but to represent, by pictorial symbols, ideas in which metaphor was desired implied a good memory and a considerable power of association on the part of the reader. As the spoken language became richer in inflections, conjugations, etc., the words acquired tenses, moods, cases, etc., which could not be pictured at all. Symbols might suffice for finite heathenism, but they would not suffice for the spiritual

[10] and infinite; a new garment in which to wrap the thoughts of men must be woven, the old proving too narrow to envelop the new expressions. A pictograph raised up two images in the mind: one seen that represented one not seen, that is, its allegorical sense. Advancing from a simple to a more complex condition, more thoughts to present, more distinctions to draw, required something more adequate than mere symbolism. Ambiguity would bring confusion and render the symbol unintelligible. To avoid this it was necessary to add a determinant or sign [ideogram] to indicate the special sense intended; but the ideas to be expressed constantly increased in number, while the characters that could be used pictorially were limited in their application—in fact, there were not enough symbols "to go round," even as today the range of human thoughts transcends the range of symbols, however wide it may be, which man has invented to express them.

At this stage the system could as yet convey little more than the simplest facts; it was a stage at which the pictures told a simple story at a glance. Later, when the picture became representative not only of an object, but also of some attribute of it, it then became a symbol that conveyed an idea as well as recording a fact, the pictograph constituting then an ideogram.

Ideographic writing came about through the increasing need for accuracy as well as expediency; and putting the principal part for the whole, or putting one thing for another, from some resemblance of qualities in the two, through constant use was to divert attention from the symbol and fix it on the significance of the thing presented. And by a further process of conventionalization the ideographs lost their ideographic character and assumed gradually the quality of syllabic signs, only then really representing sounds.

Ideas are expressed by sentences made up of parts of speech for which no symbolism, no matter how ingenious, can entirely provide. This led naturally to the use of pictures of things of different sense having names with the same sounds—a sort of rebus writing possible in any language having words of the same sound but of different meanings. To illustrate: in English the pronoun 'I' is pronounced like the word 'eye,' the word 'reign,' to rule, like the word 'rain.' The idea 'I reign' could easily be expressed in picture writing by using the pictographs for 'eye' and 'rain,' the ideogram thus becoming a phonogram and the writing phonetic. Or, to illustrate still further, the picture of a leaf would become the sign for the syllable 'leaf' wherever it might occur, and the picture of a bee would become the syllable 'be,' the pictures together forming the word 'belief.' The picture of the bee would then cease to represent the insect and would represent only the syllable 'be,' and the picture of a leaf would no longer signify leaf or foliage; the pictures would have become purely phonetic symbols, expressing words as well as ideas, the next step in their evolution toward real writing.

Let us retrace briefly the passage of the hieroglyphic characters through the stages already mentioned, and connect them in a roundabout manner with the beginnings of our own roman alphabet. First is the pictograph of the thing, next the phonogram or sign representing a sound, leading into the phonogram representing a syllable—from which alphabetic characters were easily the next step. Of the earliest phonograms representing words and syllables there were

[12] about 400, and from these the ancient Egyptians selected some 45 for alphabetic use; this number was still further reduced to 25, as the use of some characters was infrequent.

As Canon Taylor, in his book on the alphabet, observes, "All that remained to be done was to take one simple step—boldly to discard all the non-alphabetic elements, at once to sweep away the superfluous lumber, rejecting all the ideograms, the homophones, the polyphones, the syllabics, and the symbolic signs to which the Egyptian scribes so fondly clung, and so to leave revealed in its grand simplicity, the nearly perfect alphabet of which, without knowing it, the Egyptians had been virtually in possession for almost countless ages."

Unfortunately that "simple step" the Egyptians themselves never took, but continued the use of eye pictures side by side with ear pictures, combining both, instead of disregarding the pictograms and employing only fixed signs for certain sounds.

When, in the first stage of writing, a sign stood for a word, there were required, of course, as many symbols as there were words in the language. When the signs were employed to represent syllables, a great advance over the use of word signs had been made, but the method was still a clumsy device by which to express ideas. It was only when symbols finally represented the elementary sounds of the human voice that they became true letters.

When writing was entirely pictorial, in the effort to secure greater rapidity of execution simpler forms were developed, and finally, letters. The sense, in a similar manner, declined from the idea suggested by the picture into a mere syllable without concrete meaning, and finally to simple sounds corresponding to letters.

The various steps from pictures to words seem to have been taken in prehistoric times by different peoples independently. To which people must we trace our own alphabet? No doubt, ideographic signs common to several languages had in general the same meanings, but comparison of similar signs in each language would probably discover some more or less different or additional meaning or significance [except, of course, those incapable of qualitative difference*].

When used to express an idea instead of a thing, how easily the same sign might finally come in one language to have a quite different significance from that in another. Its survival, then, in one language, and its possible later disappearance from the others, might render its origin extremely difficult to trace.

The transition from pictures to ideographs to phonograms was not so pronounced as at first one might imagine. In all probability the signs were introduced so slowly and in such a manner as easily to be understood from the context—finally to become generally known and adopted without conscious thought of their original forms or their early significance.

Egyptian writing divides into three groups of characters: first, hieroglyphs in which about 700 signs preserve plainly, in their older forms, traces of their origin in rude picture writing, in turn passing through the pictographic, ideographic, and phonetic phases; second, hieratic [Gr. hieratikos, sacerdotal], a cursive abridged and conventionalized form of the hieroglyph from which it was derived, used for literary productions and employed by the priests; and third,

* The picture of a hand or an eye would, of course, represent a hand or eye regardless of the language used, whether Egyptian or other.

[14] demotic [Gr. demotikos, of the people], which arose still later [8th century B.C.], used for purposes of daily life and, though derived also from the hieroglyph, preserving even fewer traces of its derivation from picture writing than the hieratic characters.

Hieratic writing corresponds in a way to our cursive hand of correspondence, the hieroglyph to print, and the demotic notation, since it could be written rapidly and was abbreviated, to our shorthand.

Both Egyptian hieroglyphics and hieratic characters were usually written from right to left, but lines reading down were also occasionally employed.

As in the time of Darius, when proclamations and documents of importance were set forth in three languages, Babylonian, Medic, and Persian, just so in Egypt, until it fell under Roman rule, every matter of public importance was recorded in three forms, hieroglyphic, demotic, and Greek characters, and it is due to this fact that the Egyptian hieroglyphs have been deciphered, mainly through the discovery of the Rosetta Stone,* an inscribed block of black basalt found in 1799, containing fragments of 14 lines of hieroglyphics, 32 lines in demotic characters, and 54 lines of Greek.

What people, then, did take the necessary "simple step"? For one, the ancient Egyptians [whose history is fairly complete] worked out a system of writing—curious for the reason that it passed simulta-

---

*The Rosetta Stone, now in the British Museum, dates from the year 193 B.C. and is so called because it was found among the ruins of a port near the Rosetta mouth of the Nile. It is imperfect, but enough remains to give the general tenor of the inscriptions, of which the hieroglyphic and demotic portions defied decipherment until the early decades of the 19th century. Dr. Wallis Budge says that the Greek portion appears to be the original document, and the hieroglyphic and demotic versions merely translations of it.

neously through all the stages of development of a written language [15]
in which the old system was not entirely discarded or displaced by
the newer, but exhibited at once all the intermediate stages and remained to the end a system partly picture & partly alphabetic writing.

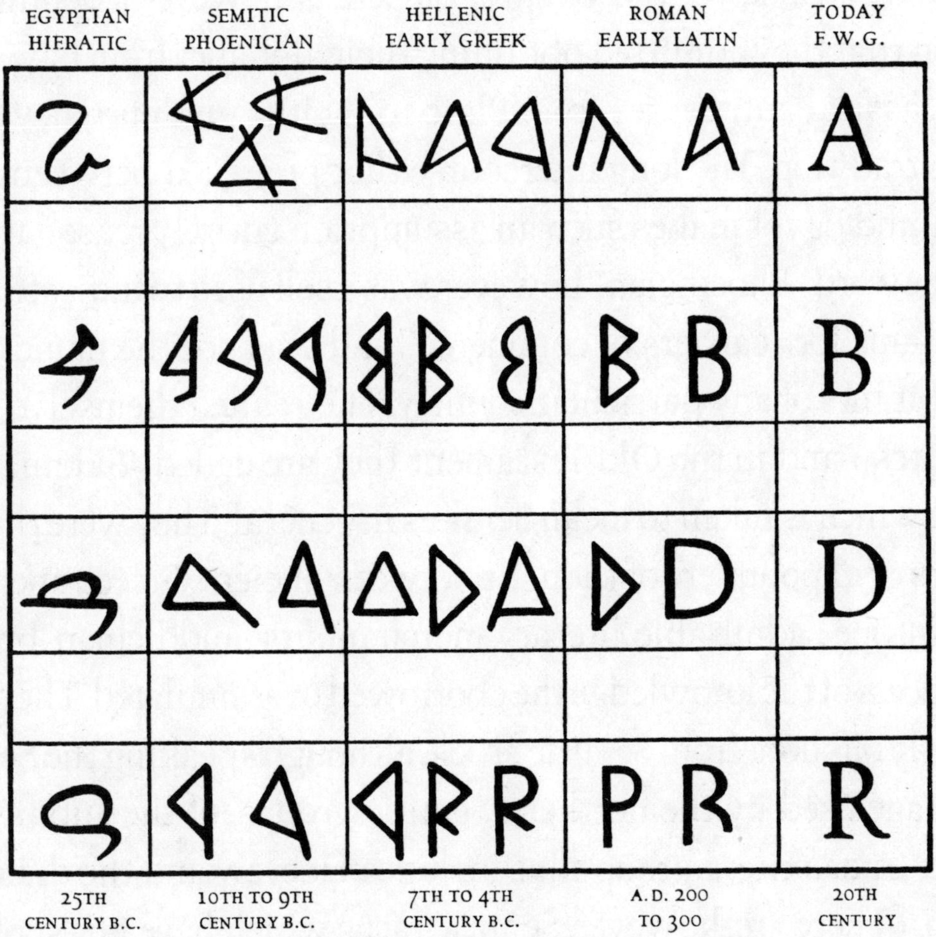

EGYPTIAN HIERATIC	SEMITIC PHOENICIAN	HELLENIC EARLY GREEK	ROMAN EARLY LATIN	TODAY F.W.G.

25TH CENTURY B.C.	10TH TO 9TH CENTURY B.C.	7TH TO 4TH CENTURY B.C.	A.D. 200 TO 300	20TH CENTURY

FIG. 3   FORMS OF LETTERS IN FIVE SUCCESSIVE ALPHABETS

Sir Edw. Maunde Thompson says that the alphabet we use today
is directly derived from the Roman; "the Roman, from a local form
of Greek; the Greek from the Phoenician." But whence was the Phoenician derived? As to this query he now says "we are not even yet in
a position to declare"; yet once it was his opinion that "in all its

[16] essential forms our alphabet can be traced to the ancient hieratic writings of the Egyptian priests of about 25 centuries B.C."

Pliny gives credit to the Phoenicians for the invention of the alphabet, but there is no direct evidence that the Phoenicians ever declared themselves the inventors. There is, however, a definite tradition that they admitted obtaining their alphabet from Egypt, and the classical authorities from Plato to Tacitus give currency to the same tradition. The long intercourse that prevailed between Phoenicia* and Egypt makes such an assumption entirely reasonable.

The word "Phoenician," however, was itself used to indicate a general name for "carriers of commerce" and was not the name of the inhabitants of any particular country. They called themselves "Canaanites," and in the Old Testament they are called "Sidonians," a name which is taken to mean Semites in general. They were the purveyors & expounders of thought between ancient Greece and modern Europe; admirable literary merchants or middlemen, but not producers of the knowledge they borrowed or assimilated. They were an early offshoot from Semitic stock, although speaking the Semitic language used by the northern Semitic groups, of the subdivision called Canaanite, a group that includes Hebrew and the dialect of Moab. [There are, however, Semitic races which have not spoken a Semitic language.]

Although the immediate prototypes of Semitic letters cannot be traced definitely to the Egyptian hieroglyphics, early forms of Phoenician inscriptions have many features in common with the oldest

---

* Phoenicia is the name given to that part of the seaboard of Syria which extends from the Nahr el-Kebir in the north to Mount Carmel in the south.

Egyptian hieratic writings. In the Old Testament certain Egyptian words are given in the Semitic form, and Semitic names of Syrian towns are found in Egyptian writings, through which the sounds severally represented by both Semitic and hieratic characters have been determined.

It is known that the Phoenicians were using an alphabet at least 900 years B.C.* and using it so purely that they must have been in possession of it for some time before that. Professor Breasted says that "while investigation has not as yet furnished proof that the Phoenician alphabet is of Egyptian origin, in some respects the development of the two alphabets is curiously parallel."

From the slab, dating about 890 B.C., known as the Moabite Stone and found near Dibon, the ancient capital of Moab, inscribed in a language closely resembling the Hebrew of the Old Testament, and from similar inscriptions dating from at least 1000 B.C., the Phoenician alphabet of 22 characters has been reconstructed in a form that must have passed through many stages of modification. It was an alphabet of consonants only, and was adopted by the Greeks, among whom the Phoenicians settled or with whom they traded. This primitive Greek alphabet was known as "Cadmean" and was so named because, according to Herodotus, Cadmus introduced the Phoenician alphabet into Greece; no certain date is known, however, at which the mythical Cadmus may have done so.

The Arameans, a highly civilized race living in the region north of Palestine, sometimes called Syrians [not to be confused, however,

* Professor Breasted says their alphabet was devised about ten centuries B.C., at which time they had given up the use of the clay tablets of Babylonia.

[18] with "Assyrians"], used an alphabetic writing which they too borrowed from the Phoenicians, with which to record business transactions in Aramaic. Their language even displaced a similar sister tongue, the Hebrew of Palestine, and many centuries later was the language spoken by Jesus and the Hebrews of his time.

Whatever the source of the Phoenician alphabet, the subsequent progress of alphabetic writing is fairly clear. Comparison of the early Greek forms with the oldest Phoenician writing demonstrates their common origin; the names of the Phoenician letters are Semitic words, each suggested by its resemblance to some particular object. Their letters were arranged in convenient order, each called after the object the name of which began with the letter to be named; for example, the Phoenician word for ox, "aleph," began with the first letter, the word for house, "beth," the second, and so on.

Arameans carried the Phoenician alphabet eastward into Asia, thus supplying the source of the Hebrew, Syriac, Arabic, Armenian, and Georgian alphabets. The Phoenicians themselves carried their alphabet westward from the Mediterranean through Greece to Europe. The Greeks learned the Phoenician alphabet and used it to write down Greek words, which they spelled with Phoenician letters. They were the first to receive the Phoenician alphabet, taking over the Semitic forms and retaining the Semitic names. They noticed the lack of signs to represent vowels, and that the Phoenician alphabet included some letters representing consonants which were not required in Greek speech. These latter they utilized as Greek vowels, changing the character of some of the letters and ultimately transposing the Semitic mode of writing from right to left. These changes, of course, evolved gradually, giving rise finally to a new alphabet known as Hellenic, and it is this alphabet that is the source of the Coptic, Greek, Cyrillic, Latin, and modern European alphabets.

One writer says that if the Semitic letters were not derived from Egypt, they must have developed either from the Hittite or the Assyrian cuneiform characters, or must have been invented by the Phoenicians—a theory not borne out by our knowledge of their national characteristics. The Babylonian script is older than the Egyptian & had in fact passed from the pictorial stage thirteen centuries before Egypt's had even reached it.

It is probable that the Phoenicians had already a long history before they appear in Syria. As Semites, quite likely they were familar with the cuneiform characters even as the early Arameans were, and it may turn out that the signs they used are modifications of the Hittite hieroglyphs. Then, too, recent discoveries indicate that Cretan and allied scripts antedate the Phoenician. The discoveries of Mr. A. J. Evans in the island of Crete have established the fact of a culture and an active intercourse between Crete, Greece, Egypt, Syria, and other countries centuries before Phoenicia trafficked there, and there have been discovered also a number of objects bearing two sorts of writing, one hieroglyphic or pictographic, the other approaching the alphabetic.*

Edw. Clodd says of the source of the Phoenician alphabet: "Putting together what is no longer conjectural, it would seem that the Phoenician alphabet was a compound from various sources....They

* "Recent discoveries prove the existence, in very remote times, in all quarters of the Mediterranean littoral and in Egypt, of symbols resembling certain alphabetical signs and preceding even the Egyptian hieroglyphics." [THOMPSON]

[20] got rid of surplus signs, of the lumber of determinatives, and the like, and invented an alphabet which, if not perfect, was of such signal value as to have been accepted by the civilized world of the past."

If by "invented" we understand simply changed shapes of characters already in existence, then history and sound tradition seem to bear out this conclusion. It may even be that our roman alphabet had not one, but many beginnings, many centers, all culminating in one entity more or less composite. It is the history of all languages, however widely they now differ, to refer themselves to a common stock, a single fountainhead, and a word once common to a number of tongues may have survived in one only. Why, then, may not the means itself of transmitting language have developed in the same manner?

Dr. Martin Sprengling, of the University of Chicago, supports, as a result of his recent decipherment of the Sinaia inscription found in 1904 by Sir Flinders Petrie in Sinai, the belief that the Greeks received their alphabet from the Semites rather than from the Phoenicians.

In all the foregoing the present writer has attempted no more than to outline briefly what seems to him the possible and logical development of written speech from the rude pictographs to the beginnings of our own alphabet, and it is not his intention to make dogmatic assertions concerning what peoples' pictographs were its original sources, since many facts are now almost completely lost in the twilight of fable.* The decipherment of the Hittite hieroglyphs and the

*The author realizes that his knowledge of paleography is slight, that he had little opportunity for original research, and that for his facts he is forced to depend chiefly upon the investigations of scholars who have made specific

establishing of their relation to other writings, the acceptance of the [21]
theory of the derivation of the Phoenician alphabet from the Babylonian cuneiform characters, the oldest script known, or possibly the
results of researches now in progress, may throw such new light on
the whole matter as to upset all previous conclusions.

studies of the origins and development
of the ancient methods of communica-
tion; nevertheless he believes that the
conclusions he presents here do form a
logical and probable story of the conventionalized evolution of our roman
alphabet from the Assyrian pictographs
to its present form. The survey is intended for readers interested only in an
outline of man's cultural development.
A more detailed discussion is not within
the scope of this study.

CHAPTER II : What Letters Are

NO WRITTEN record in any language reaches so far into the past as the language in which it is set down; indeed, language—the "pedigree of Nations," as Dr. Johnson calls it—is a more ancient and much more instructive monument than any time-eroded record that remains to us. A language is, too, the amber in which a thousand precious and subtle thoughts have been securely embedded and preserved—the very incarnation of the thought and feeling of a nation. But a language should be studied not only to gain the thoughts it reveals, but also to know it for itself alone as a sublime achievement of the human mind, and to savor the peculiar pleasure that is to be had from appreciating its beauty as a vehicle of thought.

The alphabet is a system and series of symbols representing collectively the elements of written language. Letters are the individual signs that compose the alphabet, each signifying primarily but one thing, what letter it is—its name. Each has, moreover, a secondary function, the part it plays in a word—its sound; but as this second office is not affected by any peculiarity of form or by the letter's legibility or lack of legibility, it is a function we need not consider here, since we are more concerned with the form a letter takes than with its sound.

A letter is a symbol with a definite shape and significance, indicating a single sound or combination of sounds and providing a means, through grouping, for the visible expression of words, that is, of thoughts. An individual letter, standing by itself, like a solitary note in music, has no meaning, both acquiring significance only upon association with other characters whereby a relationship is established. It may therefore, theoretically, be discussed independently; but practically it can only be treated as a part of the alphabet to which it belongs.

Originally, letters were adaptations of natural forms employed in picture writing, but by a process of evolution [actually degradation] they have become arbitrary signs with little resemblance to the symbols from which they are derived. These arbitrary shapes have passed through their periods of uncertainty and change; they have a long history and manifold associations; they are classics, and should not be tampered with, except within limits which a just discretion may allow.

An ornamental form once found is repeated, the eye grows accustomed to it and expects its recurrence; it becomes established by use; it may be associated with fundamental ideas of life and nature and is handed on and on, until finally its origin and meaning are, perhaps, lost. Just so, the pictorial significance of individual letters is so deeply buried in oblivion that special study would be necessary to resurrect their original form or meaning.

Language itself, as an organized system, was of necessity slow in developing; the next steps, the approaches toward a more or less phonetic alphabet, were equally slow; for speech existed long before it was discovered that the human voice could be represented by symbols—thus informing the brain through the eye as the voice did through the ear.

Letters are the elements of written expression, details of an accomplished system for transmitting man's conceptions or recording

[24] his activities. The roman characters we use may be considered not only for their historical development; we may also think of them for themselves alone, quite apart from their function of representing human thought visibly—that is to say, for the unique pleasure that is to be taken in the severe simplicity and beauty of their individual forms.

The history of the roman alphabet is no mere record of bloodless facts; it is as dramatic as the history of mankind, and it is true that letters, like men, have also their strange, eventful histories.

The main purpose of letters, then, is the practical one of making thoughts visible; yet they have as well a decided decorative quality, quite apart from any ornamental treatment of the separate characters. This decorative quality is one that intimately concerns the craftsman, and it will be considered later; not, however, with reference to the use of letters in ornament, but as constituting the graphic art itself. The ornamentation of the page is a subject entirely separate and distinct.

Ruskin says that "all letters are frightful things, and to be endured only upon occasion, that is to say, in places where the sense of the inscription is of more importance than external ornament." This is a sweeping statement, from which we need not suffer unduly; yet the writer doubts whether there is art in individual letters, although a delicately drawn D, O, or S may be as beautiful as any abstract lines can be. Letters in combination may be satisfying and in a well-composed page even beautiful as a whole, but art in letters consists rather in the art of arranging and composing them in an appropriate and pleasing way. The letters themselves need only be simple, well-shaped, and well-proportioned forms, well spaced and suited to the purpose intended. Nor is beauty to be sought at the expense of practical use; lettering may be beautiful and legible too, since beauty does not necessarily imply elaboration of letter forms or their ornamentation. As there is no sure recipe for design, neither is there one for the making of letters; but some knowledge of their history and development is necessary, as well as a taste enlarged by study and analysis of beautiful forms, together with an ability to feel the charm of well-designed legible pages.

All writing or lettering is a form of drawing—simple, of course. The characters of our alphabet were originally pictures or symbols, but lettering now stops short of them, since the acquisition of the ability to frame words from abstract forms makes unnecessary the ideographic or pictorial means of expression. The difference is one of degree.

As decoration is not an end in itself and must be adapted to the purpose and place for which it is planned, not being separated from the whole of which it is a part, so the individual letter form should not be considered by itself, apart from its kinsmen; for until letters are employed to form words conveying thought they are mere abstract forms with no particular significance.

Sometime in the later part of the 10th century B.C. the Phoenicians, who but a short time before had transmitted their alphabet to the Hellenes, retired from the Aegean. A rivalry for supremacy followed, in which the Greeks in Ionia contended with those in Chalcis. Out of some forty local alphabets accounted for by the political disunion of the ancient Greeks, the literal developments of the two leading

[26] groups that had divided the territory of the Mediterranean between them, alone survived. The Ionian group [including the Corinthian] was supreme in the East, while the Chalcidian or Euboean dominated Thrace and Italy. Although both Ionian and Chalcidian alphabets are derived from the Phoenician, the Ionian, in its development, deviated more from its original basis than did the Chalcidian, was adopted by Athens about 483 B.C., and at last became the classic alphabet of Greece through the intellectual supremacy of Athens.

FIG. 4   AN OSCAN INSCRIPTION

The Etruscan, Umbrian, Oscan, and Faliscan [Latin] alphabets, like the local Greek, varied also from each other by the adoption or rejection of different signs in accordance with the requirements of their respective languages; nevertheless, each of them may be traced to a common primitive type of Chalcidian alphabet. Of these Italic alphabets, the Latin alone survived; and it is the history and esthetic development of the Latin alphabet that most concern us in this brief study.

The Latin alphabet, at first practically identical with the Greek, later took an independent path as the vehicle of Greek and Roman culture; it took a simpler line of development than did the Greek, Coptic, and Slavonic alphabets [all of which were derived from the Ionian]; its eventual dominance followed naturally through the political supremacy of Rome, just as the Ionian had become dominant in Greece through the intellectual supremacy of Athens.

Thus came into use the Western [Latin] variant of the Greek alphabet which was introduced into Italy and from which evolved finally the beautiful capitals of the classic days of Roman civilization, capitals that remain, to this day, unsurpassed for beauty of form and proportion.

Lettering, the universal and most fundamental of all the arts of design, may be said to have its real beginnings in the lapidary productions of the Greeks. Their work was more monumental, but more primitive in idea, than the best of the earliest Roman work, from

FIG. 5   GREEK LETTERS FROM THE TEMPLE OF POSEIDON ON LAKE TAENARUS IN LAKONIA [476-473 B.C.]

which, however, it differed little in technical excellence. The early forms are so nearly identical with the Greek letters which precede them that a study of classic Roman capitals may just as well, and quite reasonably too, begin with those cut in stone in the first years of the Christian Era, a time when such inscriptions already had reached a high degree of excellence. It is from the Roman capitals of two thousand years ago that all the letters used by the scribes as well as the type letters of the printed books of today are derived.

The signs which compose the alphabet with which we have most to do came from Italy about two thousand five hundred years ago, and differed but little from the Greek forms from which they are derived. The Greeks, as we have already noted, were the first to receive the Phoenician alphabet in its westward course. They added separate letters to represent the vowels and changed the character of

[28] other signs, ultimately transposing the Semitic mode of writing from right to left. These changes were made slowly and the new alphabet, known as the Hellenic, is the source of the modern European alphabets, Greek and Latin, Russian and Coptic.*

The Romans added to the Greek alphabet and simplified it by dropping compound consonants and devising single letter forms for sounds previously requiring two; F instead of PH, Q for CV, etc. The

ΚΑΙΤΑΣΓΕΡΙΤΚ

FIG. 6   GREEK LETTERS FROM AN INSCRIPTION IN THE TEMPLE OF ATHENE POLIAS.
[THIRD CENTURY B.C.] ALMOST EXACT SIZE. THE LETTERS WERE
FILLED IN WITH RED AFTER CUTTING

Greek G became C in the Roman, and G came later as a separate letter distinct from C, C in turn being used for K. The Greek H stood for long E, but at the beginning of a word answered the purpose of an aspirate, the Romans using it as an aspirate only, as we do now.

A study of the alphabet leads into so many byways that it is necessary to omit much that would be of interest to the student but of no great service to the craftsman in forming a style. To trace the derivatives of the Greek involves research into languages—Coptic, Runic, Slavonic—which bear but indirectly on the shapes of the

* The Greek letter was adopted by Athens, 483 B.C. Greek manuscripts were usually written in square capitals without spaces between the words, and with but few points of punctuation. The Russian alphabet is a modification of the Cyrillic alphabet of thirty-eight characters and it remains still the most cumbersome and ungainly of modern alphabets. The Coptic alphabet is now supplanted by Arabic characters and is but little used except for liturgical purposes.

roman characters we now use; and the present work is intended primarily to deal with forms useful to the present-day craftsman.

The Latin alphabet, which to us is the most important of all, naturally shared the growing dominance of the Romans. The Empire carried its speech, and the means of recording it, to the confines of the civilized world; and the alphabet which followed the Eagles was firmly rooted by the Cross. The decadence of the Empire saw

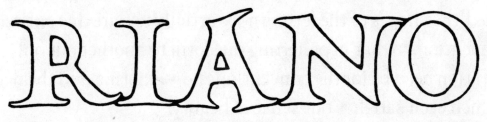

FIG. 7   ROMAN STONE-CUT CAPITALS, PROBABLY SECOND CENTURY. EXACT SIZE.
FROM A RUBBING MADE BY THE AUTHOR FROM A TABLET IN THE LOUVRE

the expansion of the Church, and the new and changing divisions of Europe were still molded by the influence of the dead and living Rome. Languages, clashing and reacting, moved toward their modern forms; 'national' scripts were developed; but the symbols borrowed from the early Chalcidian Greek colonists in Italy and then adapted to the needs of the Latins were established securely as the supreme alphabet of Christendom. Greece was the mother of modern civilization, but "Rome the Niobe of Nations" was its missionary.

CHAPTER III : Letters in General

THE HYPOTHESIS that there is an ideally correct form for each letter of the alphabet is just as erroneous as Geofroy Tory's simple assumption that there is a relation between the shapes of letters and the human body; erroneous, because the shapes of letters have been in constant process of modification from their very beginnings. Indeed, the shapes of the letters now in daily use are due entirely to a convention, so that in preferring one form to another our only consideration need be for the conventions now existing and the degree in which each satisfies our sense of beauty.

It should be kept clearly in mind that "the perfect model of a letter is altogether imaginary and arbitrary. There is a definite model for the human form. The painter, the sculptor, the architect, have their models in nature. But the man who sets himself to make an alphabet has no copy except that left him by former artists. . . . On all matters which pertain to the fashion* of his letter he has no absolute standard."

Semiscientific discussions concerning the proportions of letters began as early as 1509, first by Paciolus,† by Dürer 1525, Tory 1529, Yciar 1548, and Moxon 1676, and have continued down to the pres-

---

* The proportion of its height to its width, its serifs, its particular arcs & parallels, its weight of stem and hairlines, etc. His own eye must furnish the criterion. [REED]
† Paciolus [Lucas de Burgo], a Minorite friar, in 1494, published his important work, *Summa de Arithmetica, Geometrica, Proportioni et Proportionalita*. His writings no doubt exercised a great influence on the mathematical researches of his friend, Leonardo da Vinci, when the latter was making his studies of letters & their design, based on proportions of the human form combined with geometric figures, studies that later were further developed by Albrecht Dürer and Geofroy Tory.

ent—all with little practical or valuable result. None of the drawings or writings of these masters contain any practical hints or suggestions for use in designing new forms of letters. Rules or substitutes for the artist's hand must necessarily be inadequate, yet when set down by such men as Dürer, Tory, Serlio, and other famous masters, probably do establish and fix canons of proportion or construction that may constitute a well-laid basis upon which to found new expressions. Moxon said of letters that they "were originally invented and contrived to be made and consist of circles, arches of circles, and straight lines; and therefore those letters that have these figures entire, or else properly mixt, so as the progress of the pen may best admit, may deserve the name of true shape."

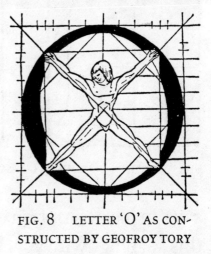

FIG. 8   LETTER 'O' AS CONSTRUCTED BY GEOFROY TORY

But these selfsame curves, arcs of circles, straight lines, also make up letter forms that we do not always consider to be of "true shape"; nor is it possible to entertain the opinion that all letters, although actually composed of these very elements, will necessarily submit to analysis or be reducible to set rules of formation that will make easier the creation of new forms. Such an analysis can, at best, only fix and permit the reproduction of the same form at another time; and even then the quality of life and freedom in the original will be in large part lost in the reproduction. The mere blending together of geometrical elements common to all letter forms, good or bad, is not enough; 'true shape' is something more subtle than geometry. The three letters, n, o, and p, shown on the next page, have been carefully

[32] redrawn from a sheet* in the possession of the writer, but whose work they are or from what book they are taken he does not know. In drawing these letters, simple as they appear to be, the author found that it was necessary to do more than use straightedge, bow pen, or other such instrument; some lines had to be shaped, as Dürer

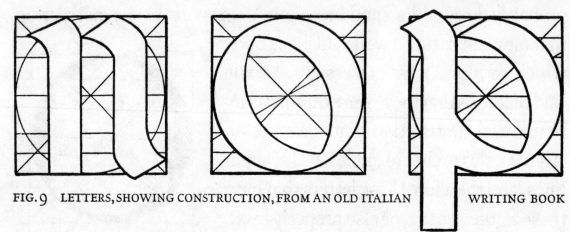

FIG. 9   LETTERS, SHOWING CONSTRUCTION, FROM AN OLD ITALIAN   WRITING BOOK

says† in his description of the letter O, "to a juster proportion," and this shaping "with your hand" is often the nub of the whole matter.

In both Greek and Latin paleography large letters are called "majuscules" and are of two kinds. First are capitals, originally cut in stone and made chiefly by strokes meeting at angles, curves being avoided except where the shapes of the letters absolutely required curves, as angular characters are more easily cut in stone or metal; and second, uncials, which are a modification of capitals, curves being freely introduced since they are readily inscribed with a pen.

* The gift of Mr. Harry Peach, Leicester, England, a courtesy the writer begs to acknowledge.

† "Now O you shall make this way in its square. Set in the square the diameter c. b. and bisect it in the point e., so that e. may form a middle point between the two points f. and g. which are to be your two centres; and from each let a circle be described touching two sides of the square; and where the circles cut one another, there *with your hand you must shape the slender outline of the letter to a juster proportion.*" [DÜRER; see fig. 10]

A comprehensive study of the history and development of the characters that finally evolved into the familiar lower-case forms of today would seem to require a knowledge of the Greek and Latin tongues. We may, however, with only a slender knowledge of those languages, study for themselves the forms employed to write them,

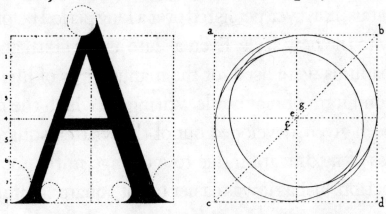

FIG. 10   PROPORTIONS OF ROMAN CAPITALS.
FROM DRAWINGS BY DÜRER

and trace with little difficulty the transition of the square capitals first used into uncials, later into a mixed hand made up of uncials and occasional minuscules—which, without doubt, were mere interpolations of letters from the cursive hand of the time—and developing finally into the half uncials which are the direct forerunner of the minuscule book hand from which our lower-case letters come.

Early Latin writing [in majuscules], as we have just noted, is divided into two kinds: capitals, & uncial writing. The first employed capitals which are themselves again of two kinds, namely, square and rustic. The written square capitals in general are more formal and approximate closely the forms cut in stone, the angles by preference being right angles, the tops, bases, and extremities finished with finer strokes or serifs. The rustic capitals are more negligent in

[34] pattern, less finished as completed letters, and, although accurately shaped, can be written more rapidly than capitals.

By the end of the fourth century, capitals, through the corrupting influence of the cursive writing then in use, had changed their shapes sufficiently to indicate the beginnings of a new variety of letter, the uncial; capitals, however, persisted over a long period before entirely giving way to the new style. Even as late as the sixth and seventh centuries capitals were used for the manuscripts of literary texts.

The second form of majuscule writing, to which the name "uncial" has been given, developed out of the written square capitals by a process of modification due to a change in the tool used for their production. Just as it was easier to cut square capitals in stone or metal, so was it easier to avoid right angles by employing curves when forming letters with a reed or pen on a material more or less soft. Uncial writing, then, is essentially a round hand, presenting curved forms in its characteristic letters, and leading naturally into a modified form in which mixed uncial and minuscule letters are employed; the beginnings of our lower-case forms, a, d, e, h, m, are characteristic letters.

In early Greek writing the ordinary character used was the uncial, and it sometimes retained more or less of the lapidary capital form. But at no period did the Greek uncial develop so fully as the Latin form.

Majuscule writing, both capital and uncial, represents the literary script of its period and was comparatively limited in range. Running by its side was the ordinary cursive hand in general use; under certain conditions, characters from the cursive writing occasionally would invade the majuscule writing, which would then exhibit minuscule forms proper only to the cursive hand. In the writing done on waxed tablets in nonliterary scripts, a mingling of capitals and minuscules prevailed from the first, and there are indications that later the same mingling was allowed in literary writings. In the text of the Epitome of Livy [third century] minuscule letters are interspersed with the uncial forms, their regularity and apparent ease of writing clearly suggesting that this mixed hand was even then an ordinary practice. The writing shows distinct minuscule forms of the letters b, a, m, r, and f, sometimes uncial, occasionally minuscule.

Reference to various manuscripts shows that the number of minuscule forms included with uncials in the early examples of mixed writing depended somewhat on the taste of the writer. The mixed hand passed through various phases, reaching soon a fully developed condition in which the minuscule element asserted itself so strongly that few purely uncial forms remained; at this stage it acquires a recognized position, it becomes the half-uncial hand, and marks clearly the change from capitals to minuscules or small letters. The half-uncial literary hand was the basis for the beautiful national book hands of Ireland and Britain. In its full development, half-uncial writing might almost pass for a large minuscule hand, owing to the large proportion of the forms afterward found in the minuscule hand of the Carolingian period, and, indeed, it has sometimes been termed the pre-Carolingian [or, pre-Caroline] minuscule.

The chief difference between inscriptional characters and MS. letters lies in the fact that the stone-cut forms are compound, that is, they are built up, a part at a time, and not made by single sweeping

[36] strokes of a pen or brush. They were probably designed in situ by a master writer, who was able, by incessant practice with a flat stiff brush, to draw or write rapidly, the actual cutting or fixing of the letters probably being left to one accustomed to work in stone.

Minor refinements, and more careful cutting of the curves and serifs, gave a quality that was later carried naturally into written forms—the square capitals of the fourth-century MSS., which are merely a pen-drawn variety of the lapidary capitals and retain a strong resemblance to them. Manuscript letters, however, were simple written shapes in which the varying widths of the lines composing them were in strict relation to the breadth and angle of the pen used, the mere changing of its direction producing striking results in the character and development of the letters. When letters were written with a broad pen or formed by strokes of a brush, the relation of the thick and thin lines was not a result of deliberate thought, but rather of a natural handling of the tool employed. No pencil-outlined forms, later filled in with ink or color, can give so vivid a quality of life, variety, and harmony as those produced directly and spontaneously.

CHAPTER IV: The Development of the Roman Capital

EMERSON somewhere has said that "language is fossil poetry," meaning, of course, that just as some curious insect, a beautiful leaf, or graceful fern, extinct for ages, is now bound up permanently with the stone & saved from the fate which otherwise would have fallen to it, just so in words, the beautiful thoughts, the imagination and feeling of men long since gone, have been preserved to us and forever. Less figuratively, but even more truly, the earliest forms of the Roman alphabet were, in very fact, crystallized and saved to us in the stone-cut inscriptions wrought by the Greeks of yesterday, and those shapes, transplanted by the early Chalcidian Greek colonists into Italy, provide the immediate sources of the alphabet we know and use today.

From a tablet dug up at Sigeum, a promontory near the site of ancient Troy [discovered by William Sherard, then English consul at Smyrna], we have in early Greek characters probably the oldest literal inscription extant. The writing on it discloses an interesting deviation from the usual custom of most of the Eastern nations: the first line, beginning at the left, reads to the right, the following line commences at the right and runs to the left, and the characters are likewise reversed, each line beginning at the side at which the preceding line ends, and so on. Probably this method of writing, called boustrophedon,* was in vogue but for a short time, as an inscription on the base of the Colossus at Delos and also an inscription on

*As an ox turns at the end of the furrow in plowing. *Bous*, ox; *strophe*, turning.

BEAUTY
IS THE VISIBLE
EXPRESSION
OF MAN'S
PLEASURE IN
LABOR
C D G J K Q
W Z &

FIG. 11 'FORUM' CAPITALS BY F.W.G. [1911]

one of the Tripods at Thebes, both practically contemporary with the Sigean fragment, read from left to right only. The letters are cut on a pillar of white marble, nine feet high, two feet wide, and eight inches thick, which quite probably supported a bust or statue of Hermocrates, whose name appears in the text of the inscription. The writing itself presents a specimen nearly three thousand years old.

In the British Museum there is a brass signet, found near Rome, the appearance of which indicates very great age. The signet probably was intended for stamping or printing its owner's signature on documents that were written on parchment or other substance used for receiving writing. On its face, which is about two inches in length and four-fifths of an inch wide, letters of good proportion [in reverse] are engraved in relief within a border line or rim. A

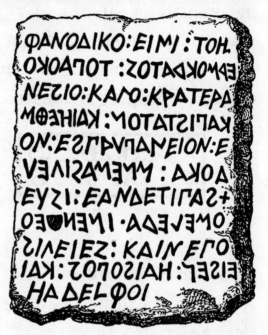

FIG. 12 SIGEAN TABLET, ILLUSTRATING BOUSTROPHEDON

[TRANSLATION]

I am Hermocrates, the son of Phanodicus, of this Promontory, and I have presented in the Prytaneum a cup with a stand and wine strainer, as a monument to Sigeans. If, then, on any account I am troubled, I go to the Sigeans, and Aesopus, and my brethren have erected this monument for me.

ring, which serves as a handle, is attached to the back of the plate. The letters are capitals huddled together with little punctuation, in the usual style of the old Roman inscriptions. They spell "CICAECILI HERMIAS. SN.," or, as we would print it today, "C. J. CAECILI HERMIAE SIGNUM," which translated is, "The seal of Caius Julius Caecilius Hermias." Of

[40] Hermias himself we know almost nothing. He used the signet to save himself the trouble of writing, or possibly to hide his inability to write. The stamp quite plainly was intended for printing or stamping on materials used for writings rather than for impressions in wax or metal and is significant in this connection as prefiguring the art of printing that was to come many years later. That it was intended for printing is indicated by the fact that the background or

THE SIGNET AS IT APPEARS   THE SIGNET AS STAMPED

FIG. 13   SIGNET OF CAIUS JULIUS CAECILIUS HERMIAS

field, that is, the part cut away to leave the border and letters in relief, is very rough and uneven in depth, while the letters and the border line are smooth and exactly the same height. An impression of this sigil in wax would produce letters sunk below the surface of the plastic material, & the raised surface around them would be rough while the raised surface that would show when impressed would, of course, be smooth in a seal engraved for impressions in wax.

For nearly two thousand years the roman capital has held the supreme place among all letters for beauty and character. The Italian typefounders in the fifteenth century sought out fine examples in MSS. as models for their minuscules; for their majuscules they studied & attempted to reproduce the capitals from the monumental Roman inscriptions. Their fine traditions have in large part been lost. Examples extant show that the earliest forms of the lapidary Roman capitals were roughly shaped and without the thick & thin ſtrokes that add materially to their legibility and diſtinction. In the first century B.C. the increasingly common practice of cutting monumental inscriptions led to more highly developed forms, & many even now show indications that the letters were first carefully outlined or painted in before cutting, afterward to be filled in with the same color as was used in the preliminary outlining—a conclusion suggeſted by the accuracy that is characteriſtic of inscriptions cut in bronze or ſtone. Letters cut in bronze were occasionally made more diſtinct by filling in the incised lines with white lead. Sometimes, on large public monuments, separate letters of bronze or lead were affixed to the ſtone with rivets, and for some of these it is only by the positions of the rivet holes remaining after the letters forming the inscription had fallen that it has been possible to reſtore the original text.

Of all the examples remaining to us, the inscription at the base of the Trajan Column at Rome, cut about A.D. 114, is probably the fineſt in character. This column, one hundred forty-seven feet high, erected by the senate & people of Rome, is composed of thirty-four blocks of marble and is covered with a spiral band of bas-reliefs illuſtrating the Dacian wars, almoſt the only record of these wars surviving. When first erected, it was crowned by a ſtatue of Trajan holding a gilt globe, but the ſtatue had fallen long before Pope Sixtus V replaced it with the ſtatue of St. Peter which now surmounts the column. The base forms a sepulchral chamber intended to receive the imperial remains, & it is believed by some that the ashes of the Emperor, in their golden urn, might even now be found buried in front of the column—which was put up while Trajan was ſtill

[42] living,—as it was the custom to preserve the imperial ashes in such an urn upon an altar in front of the sepulchral chamber. Of the column itself, Hawthorne said, "It is a great, solid fact of the Past, making old Rome actually visible to the touch and eye; and no study of history, nor force of thought, nor magic of song, can so vitally assure us that Rome once existed, as this sturdy specimen of what its rulers and people wrought."

An examination of the letters composing the inscription at the base of the column shows that the vertical, horizontal, oblique, and curved strokes vary considerably in thickness, and with no absolute regularity; they show also that the swelling of the curves occurs above and below centers, according as they are on the right or left sides, & that the letters vary considerably in their individual widths.

This variety in width of lines was in no way made necessary by any demand of material or of cutting tool, but since the natural handling of pen or brush will actually produce just such variety of line, it is reasonable to assume that the use of pen or brush influenced very strongly the shaping of the lapidary characters, if indeed they did not really determine the actual forms. The shapes they take in general and their proportions are, therefore, those of the pen-drawn letters, but their character is that of the cutting tool used to produce them—a significant point to bear in mind.

It is frequently remarked of the Roman capitals that there seems to be no good reason for the ungainly disparities in their various widths.* To the writer, however, there is a fundamental reasonableness in their peculiar proportions [of which varying widths are an essential feature] that marks for him a close relation between these

* See figure 14, page 45, below.

capitals & their far-off Phoenician originals; nor are those proportions and widths merely a matter of conscious or elaborate design. There is, too, a profound consistency in the Roman alphabet as a whole—a relationship between the individual letters that compose it, owing to the following of a sound tradition by craftsmen free from conscious effort toward beauty. Those ancient craftsmen were much more anxious for consistency in the form & appearance of their work than concerned with the question of widths of individual letters.

The earliest syllabic or alphabetic signs that evolved from the Egyptian pictographs by a process of conventionalization & simplification retained, in some degree and for a long time, traces of their pictorial origin. The spaces required for the representation of the different objects employed for the pictographs naturally varied just as the actual objects themselves varied in proportion or shape; the more abstract symbols which grew out of the pictographs through rapid writing and abbreviation became purely conventional forms the pictorial significance of which was eventually lost or forgotten. These forms became traditional and were adopted by the Phoenicians as the basis of their alphabet; the spaces required to express the conventional forms might easily have varied in the same way, since the abstract symbols themselves, no doubt, kept more or less closely to the varying widths of their pictorial originals. Therefore, the early Greek & Roman stonecutters, heirs to the genius of Phoenicia, produced letters as of forms the widths of which were already established for them; these they modified or altered to their own use only just sufficiently to meet the exigencies of the technical requirements of the tools employed in their production. Nevertheless,

[44] neither the materials in which they worked nor the tools employed for cutting had, at any time, more than a modifying influence over the actual shapes of the letters themselves—forms with which the workmen were already familiar and which under their hands gradually developed, by imperceptible refinements, into letter forms especially suitable to the tools employed. There was no material change or loss of their original or generic characters, the essential shapes, in which varying widths were an important detail, remaining practically unaltered.

The writer's theory seems amply borne out by a comparison of the early Greek letters with their Phoenician originals: nearly all the Greek forms follow closely the widths of the characters from which each was derived. But whether or not the Phoenician characters follow, likewise, the widths of their hieratic originals, or the hieratic characters follow the widths of the pictographs they conventionalize, the writer is not able to ascertain, the materials for a careful examination of all the transitional forms not being within his reach.

Moreover, the process of modification from pictures to letter symbols covered a long period ; nor did the forms, at once, assume fixed shapes, but varied with the conceptions of every different maker of them, the nature of the tool he employed, and the material on which he fashioned them. The forms themselves became trite and ordinary, and, as handed on and on, gradually grew away from their pictorial forebears until finally they no longer bore any resemblance to, or even suggestion of, the forms that inspired them, their pictorial significance by then being lost and too deeply buried in oblivion to make resurrection easy. After all, it is not really necessary to press the theory beyond the earliest Phoenician alphabet [1000 B.C.], since Phoenician letters seem to have been the actual final literal development of the constantly changing ideographic symbols through the hieratic and demotic writings; and it is on the widths of those forms that the writer chiefly bases his suggestion, in the absence, as far as he is aware, of any specific statement elsewhere regarding the matter.

ABDEGNRS

FIG. 14   STONE-CUT CAPITALS FROM THE TRAJAN COLUMN. [A.D.114]

Our nature seems to appreciate variety, a quality inherent in Roman letters; while more than half of the Roman letters are made of straight lines, the others contain curves that complement them and supply the grace demanded. Of Greek letters, two-thirds are straight-lined, with a paucity of curves. Almost every Roman letter has individuality—an inscription in Roman capitals is full of vital touches.

The curves in the Trajan capitals are not simple geometrical lines, but are carefully considered quantities which impart a character to the forms that no mechanical construction can possibly give. Drawn freely, untrammeled by bow pen, straightedge, or mechanical rule in the pursuit of distinction and style, each new line leads on to new difficulties to be overcome, to new subtleties of form, & to constant varieties by each change of taste or fancy. So far as we of today are concerned, the Trajan alphabet, in its spontaneity, is primal.

The capitals shown on this page were carefully drawn from photographs of the Trajan Column at Rome.

[46] The great merit of Roman capitals is simplicity; every useless & meaningless line has been eliminated. The letters vary in shape and proportion, & to bring out their full beauty requires a nice discrimination in the spacing and combining of their irregular forms.

For years after the fall of Rome, Latin lettering was retrograde, but with the advent of the Renaissance, pure classic forms of the ancients were revived; and the Italian Renaissance, it may be said, was the "golden age" of lettering. The Renaissance artists seem indeed to have grasped the spirit of classicism, and their productions acquired a sense of refinement and grace that was not always present in the earlier work. In Persia, a sentence written by a master of calligraphy is treasured as we might treasure a drawing by Holbein; the severe purity of the lapidary letters of the Renaissance produces a thrill of pleasure in the same way that the subtle proportions of a classic column move men to a desire for emulation. These artists of the Renaissance, however, added little to the essential forms already established by the early craftsmen, so that their work needs no further mention here.

Through all the centuries since the first use of Roman capitals, scribes and printers have been developing uncials, half uncials, capitals, lower-case letters, and italics; the original form of the Roman majuscule from which each of these later forms is derived has been retained in all its essentials and still holds an organic place in the books and inscriptions of today. Especially is this apparent in the stone-cut inscriptions of the present. Other forms of lettering used in common commercialism have suffered, yet the fine tradition of the lapidary capital still persists. Forms based on metal types or on hand lettering often seem mean, trivial, and without dignity when inscribed in ſtone. Much modern work seems to lack the spirit of delight in fine craftsmanship so evident in the old work.

Letters, to be classic, need not be caſt in Greek or Latin mold; if they are expressed clearly, as a Greek or Roman might have rendered them, with entire freedom from whims and with a realization of the necessity for direɛtness, no frigid adherence or pedantic prejudice for the Greek or Latin forms themselves is essential. Classicism, therefore, is not the mere reproduɛtion of those creations, but, inſtead, is the craftsman's individual reëxpression, in the spirit of the classical, of the thought underlying those ancient charaɛters.

SYRIO

FIG. 15   LETTERS FROM AN INSCRIPTION IN THE CHURCH OF S. ANASTASIA, ROME [A.D. 1261], SHOWING AN UNUSUAL FORM OF AN INSCRIPTIONAL 'Y,' A LETTER OF LATE IMPORTATION INTO THE LATIN AND ORIGINALLY USED ONLY IN WORDS BORROWED FROM THE GREEK. FROM A RUBBING MADE BY THE AUTHOR

CHAPTER V : Letters Before Printing

AT FIRST the Romans used two varieties of characters: capitals & cursive. The capitals were square-shaped and were used for inscriptions, and for lines requiring emphasis or prominence, as we use capitals nowadays, and for writings of importance. Figure 16 shows some square capitals carefully drawn from a fragment of the

FLORIBVS'ETDV CVMTEGRALYP

FIG. 16   SQUARE CAPITALS, FROM VERGIL'S AENEID. [FOURTH CENTURY]

Aeneid of Vergil, written on vellum about the end of the fourth century. The letters are rather heavy and not very compact, and with but little spacing between the words. The only mark of punctuation is a kind of comma raised to the top of the line of writing. F is made slightly taller than E, as also L and occasionally I.*

The cursive or running characters which are the originals of our lower-case types or minuscules were used for correspondence or for documents in which more formal writing was not necessary or desirable. This script, offering little of practical use, is not shown here.

* The early Roman scribe based his written forms on the stone-cut letters. Note the similarity of such letters as B, C, P, R, in figure 16, and the same letters as represented in the author's "Hadriano" type [fig. 41, p. 86].

From the fourth century to the seventh, four principal types of [49] character were in use—the capital of the earliest documents; the uncial, almost exclusively predominant after the fifth century; the cursive script in its various modifications as employed for purposes

FIG. 17   RUSTIC WRITING OF THE FIFTH CENTURY

of everyday use; and finally a modified uncial, which prepared the way for the later minuscule.

The early form, whether Greek or Roman, was the square capital with its relatively few curved lines, which, when rounded, was used for manuscript writing and called "rustic" [fig. 17], as it was some- what more fanciful or flexible than the form used for cutting in stone or for fine writing.

The square capital has persisted in the lines and the proportions crystallized in its earliest use; it is the monumental letter, simple and direct and bold. The capitals inscribed on the base of the Trajan

[50] Column at Rome are as legible to our eyes as if carved but yesterday instead of more than eighteen hundred years ago. [Facing page 5 is shown the inscription on the Arch of Titus, erected at Rome in the first century of the Christian Era, set in "Forum" capitals, a type face based on the ancient lapidary characters.] Each of the full-page plates, pp. 105 ff., shows a large letter from the Trajan Column.

The uncial form [described in chapter iii] was of fewer lines and more rounded than the rustic, which the copyists found somewhat difficult to execute easily, although even this latter style of letter was composed of fewer strokes than the square capital. The uncial is important to us principally because it helps to explain a later form widely different from the original square capital. Uncials made their appearance in Italy about the second century, but came into general use in the fourth. They were based mainly on the square capitals, were very simple in form, and indicate clearly the firm use of a soft reed or quill pen.

Uncials are typically pen-drawn capitals & differ from capitals only in the letters A, D [ð], E [ϵ], G [ɢ], H, M, T [τ], Q, and V. None have been found that are more than five-eighths of an inch in height, although the name is derived from uncia, an inch. Paleographers call them "majuscules," that is, large letters.

The nature of the uncial form does not permit it to be made very small, or rather, perhaps, if it is made small it ceases to be an uncial; in the oldest books many were so large that comparatively few could find place even on a large page. This waste of space and the increasing difficulty in procuring parchment compelled a reduction in the size of characters used.

The illustration shows some Roman uncials of the seventh cen- tury; note the letters A, D, E, H, and M, which differ most from the original models. Compare also with the rustic capitals of the fifth century [fig. 17, p. 49].

When bookmaking became more general and the need grew for a greater number of books, the scribes found it necessary to increase

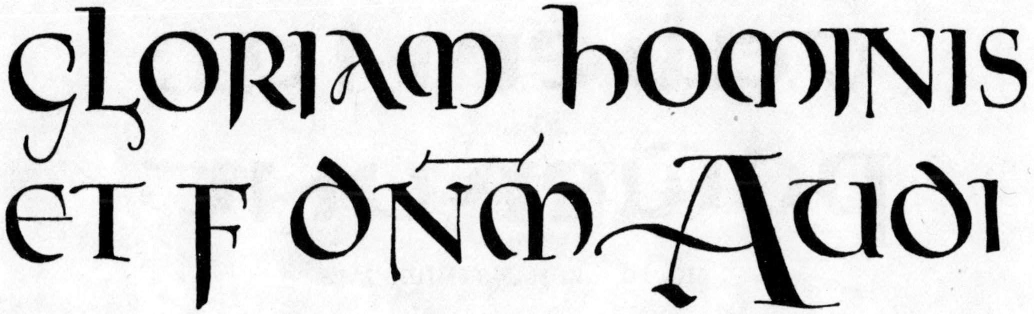

GLORIAM hOMINIS ET F ONM AUDI

FIG. 18   ROMAN UNCIALS OF THE SEVENTH CENTURY, WITH RUSTIC INITIAL.
FROM THE SPECULUM OF ST. AUGUSTINE

their product. Neither the uncial previously in use nor the cursive script enabled them to meet the new conditions. The uncial writing, beautiful as it was, was too slow,* and the cursive too ordinary for good book work; therefore a compromise hand developed which was more readily written than the capital book hand & more legible than the ordinary hand of business. This new hand was written in small characters which came to be called "minuscules." When completely developed, it superseded all other writing for books, except for Bible manuscripts or lives of the saints, which were still issued in the older uncial character. At first, little distinction was made between the minuscule forms and the capitals from which they devel-

* Sometimes indicated by the appearance   scribe allowed his writing to take on a of impatience at ends of lines, where the   more cursive character.

oped, but from the more rapid writing of capitals certain modifications took place, finally evolving an entirely new character, which reached its relative perfection in the tenth and eleventh centuries, & then degenerated with use, as do all scripts. Figure 19 shows an enlargement of some of the Roman semiuncials, of historical interest rather than of any artistic value.

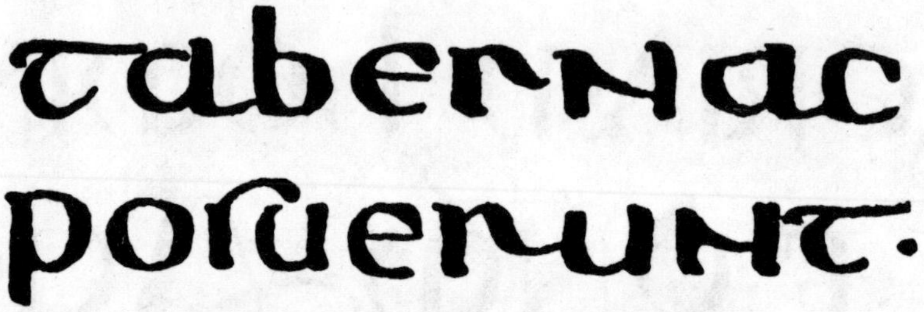

tabernac

posuerunt.

FIG. 19   ROMAN SEMIUNCIALS

multos afgr

FIG. 20   IRISH SEMIUNCIALS

Pater hofter qui

FIG. 21   ENGLISH SEMIUNCIALS

Cursive or running characters gave rise to a variety of handwritings, of which the Irish "semiuncial" is the most important. No Irish hand is known on which it could have been formed, yet in the sixth century Ireland was the chief school of Western calligraphy, & in the seventh the Irish writing had attained an excellence so great that it has since been unrivaled. It is said that Ireland borrowed the forms for her handwriting from the manuscripts which the Roman missionaries brought there in the fifth century. These manuscripts were usually written in a half-uncial character, that is, a mixture of uncials and minuscules or smaller letters. The illustration [fig. 20] shows typical letters of the Irish semiuncial writing and is from the Book of Kells, a volume written about the end of the seventh century, decorated with wonderful initials.

With the revival of learning which took place in the eighth century, the Emperor Charlemagne compelled the employing of skilled writers,* who reintroduced the smaller Roman character, the use of which had declined with the decadence of the Roman Empire. From their writing was derived the so-called Caroline minuscule, which was specially developed at the famous school at Tours founded by the Englishman Alcuin, the learned friend of Charlemagne. Alcuin, trained in the schools of Northumbria, was for some time Abbot of the Convent of St. Martin at Tours, and under his guidance the school became celebrated for the excellence of its calligraphy. He took for his models the best features of the classical hands of the sixth century, added suggestions of contemporary French & Italian lettering, and produced a half uncial and minuscule of great beauty, more legible than any earlier script.

From the eighth to the thirteenth century, the Caroline hand gradually developed in different directions and its influence extended throughout Europe—in fact, throughout the civilized world. Devel-

* Charlemagne ordered that "every abbot, bishop and count should keep in permanent employment a qualified copyist, who must write correctly, using the Roman letters only, and that every monastic institution should maintain a room known as a *scriptorium*." Alcuin entreated the monks to zealousness in their scribal work. He said: "It is a most meritorious work, more beneficial to the health than working in the fields, which profits only a man's body, whilst the labor of the copyist profits his soul." It was both piety and art.

[54] oped in different parts of the Empire, it acquired varying national characteristics, with a general tendency to a loss of breadth and a substitution of a regular angularity in the curves, owing possibly to the imitations of the coarse characters of monkish manuscripts. At

DIALOGI·I·

UBIMULTITUDO homi

NUM INSPERATA OCCURRIT

audire allum descimar

tiniuirtitibus locuturo

Ubipuellam duodecennem ab

uteromutam curauit

Ubioleum subeius benedicto

FIG. 22   SQUARE CAPITALS, UNCIALS, AND MINUSCULES IN A CAROLINE MS.
[TOURS, NINTH CENTURY]

the end of the twelfth century, when a period of decadence set in, a class of letters was produced to which the name "Gothic" has been given. Curves almost entirely gave way to straight lines, at first of scarcely varying thickness but gradually emphasizing the thickness of the perpendicular strokes while evolving a fine or thin line for the sloping ones. By the end of the thirteenth century, new forms and essential changes in alphabets had arisen out of the changing Caroline minuscule, brought about by the greater facility acquired by continuous practice. The letter we call "lower-case" was the final step in evolution from the Caroline hand, but it did not reach the definite and fixed form which has become familiar to our eyes until after the invention of printing.* Lower-case forms were rare in the fourth century, more common in the eighth, and almost universal in the tenth. Let us go over the foregoing and set down more concretely the de-

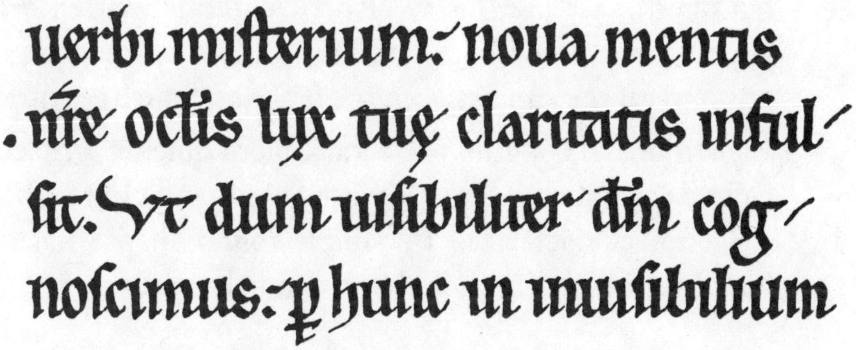

uerbi mifterium: noua mentis
. nre octis lyx tug claritatis inful
fit. Vt dum ufibiliter din cog
nofcimus: p hunc in muufibilium

FIG. 23   ENGLISH WRITING OF THE TWELFTH CENTURY

velopment of the roman alphabet, including mention in proper sequence of the national hands, the Gothic letter, & first types, which will be treated more fully hereafter.

FIRST : CAPITALS

LAPIDARY LETTERS   a The Roman capital as cut in stone, of which the inscription on the base of the Trajan Column is the finest example. Note that a characteristic of this alphabet consists in the varying widths of the letters, of which some are square and some round—the square having the horizontal lines at right angles to the vertical strokes. [See plates, pp. 105 ff.]

MANUSCRIPT FORMS   b Square Roman capitals, which, carefully written, became the formal literary hand, and were used until about the end of the fifth century for important books. The external angles invariably are right angles, and the curves regular and symmetrical [fig. 16].

* It is an interesting fact that the first roman lower-case types have not been surpassed, probably because type designers continue, with myopic industry & rigid obstinacy, to copy copies of copies *ad infinitum* [*ad nauseam*].

FIRST : CAPITALS—*Continued*

MANUSCRIPT
FORMS

c Rustic capitals, a variety of square capitals used in manuscripts of the fifth, sixth, and seventh centuries, less formal than the carefully drawn Roman letter on which they are based. They were used for years as ornamental letters for titles, etc., after they had gone out of ordinary use [fig. 17]. Rustic capitals written between the years 31 B.C. and A.D. 79 are known, but no examples have survived to fill the gap between the first and fourth centuries.

d Roman uncials or true pen forms, more quickly written than the square capital on which they are based, and clearer than the rustic form, characterized by simple round shapes natural to pen handling [fig. 18]. Perfected in the fourth century.

SECOND : CURSIVE

MANUSCRIPT
FORMS

a Roman half uncials, which were mixed uncial and cursive forms adopted by scribes for quick and easy writing and which mark the change from capitals to small letters [fig. 19].

b Irish half uncials based on the Roman forms [fig. 20].

c English half uncials modeled on the Irish, later developing into a pointed writing, a result of slanting the pen [fig. 21].

d The Caroline minuscule, a revival of the round, open, earlier Roman forms [fig. 22], which under Alcuin took on a simple & graceful form that gradually excluded all other hands. In the eleventh century it assumed a more finished form and continued to improve until in the twelfth century its beauty was unsurpassed. In England the writing of this century is particularly fine.

THIRD : THE NATIONAL HANDS

MANUSCRIPT
FORMS

1 Lombardic or national hand of Italy, founded on the old cursive.

2 Visigothic, or national hand of Spain.

3 Merovingian, or national hand of France.

4 Celtic, or national hand of Ireland, based on Roman semiuncials.

FOURTH : THE SO-CALLED "GOTHIC"

MANUSCRIPT
FORMS

A written form which evolved from the national hands, but which became a distinct style in the twelfth century. It is not properly called "Gothic," as it was not derived from the Goths but was in fact the bad writing of monkish scribes, who endeavored to conceal their lack of skill by a sort of ornamentation.

FIFTH : PRINTING

TYPES

a The Gothic black-letter of Gutenberg and the early printers.

b The transitional form used by Sweynheim and Pannartz, the German printers at Subiaco [near Rome].

c The well-nigh perfect roman form developed by Nicolas Jenson, the Frenchman who printed at Venice.

d The Aldine or italic, by Aldus Manutius, the great Italian printer at Venice. It was at first called "Venetian" in Italy, and "Cursiv" in Germany and Holland, where it was copied almost at once; in France it was called "italic," the name by which it is still known to French and English readers. All these type forms are dealt with fully in another chapter.

chriſtus agd

FIG. 24   GOTHIC TYPES OF EHRHARD RATDOLT [ENLARGED]

FIG. 25 'LOMBARDIC' [PAINTED] CAPITALS BY F.W.G.

CHAPTER VI : The National Hands

WITH the decline of the Roman Empire, the writings of other nations rose in importance and we see a variety of characters which the evolution of national hands brought about. The text hands in use in western Europe up to the age of Charlemagne may be classified into four kinds, each developing its own form but later all merging gradually into one, which we now call "Gothic."

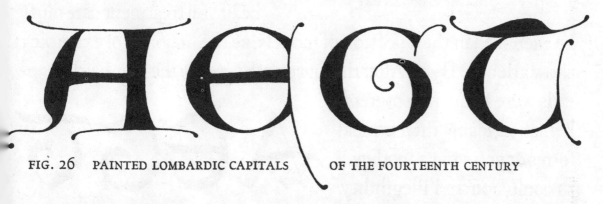

FIG. 26   PAINTED LOMBARDIC CAPITALS   OF THE FOURTEENTH CENTURY

First, Lombardic, or the national hand of Italy, which was a development of the uncial and was first used in northern Italy. The Lombardic character is a most useful and interesting form and presents less of the fixed quality of the Roman. There are many & wide variations of it as developed by the scribes in different countries. It was the favorite form selected for initials & versals in manuscripts, which were usually painted in, in colors and gold, the solidity of the body strokes making it especially adaptable for this purpose. At its best this Lombardic letter preserves much of the feeling of the uncials of the sixth and seventh centuries.

Lombardic capitals do not combine well in words or sentences, although they are frequently so misused. Occasionally, where the

[60] decorative quality sought is of more importance than easy legibility, they offer an opportunity for richness difficult to attain with other forms. If drawn carefully and well spaced, there is no reason why they should not be used, except for the reader's lack of familiarity with them.* For ecclesiastical printing they are particularly suitable. Though the Lombardic capital is capable of really beautiful treatment, care must

FIG. 27   LOMBARDIC WRITING OF THE
THIRTEENTH CENTURY

be exercised in the selection of models, as the majority of examples show a debased type. After the fourteenth century the Lombardic capitals were frequently overembellished, losing their typical forms & showing a tendency to confusion and illegibility. Those shown in figure 26 are not too ornate. The existing

FIG. 28   LOMBARDIC CAPITALS OF THE
THIRTEENTH CENTURY

type forms of the Lombardic character mostly lose all the freedom of the hand-drawn letter and seldom grace the page. In the tenth and eleventh centuries this form of letter attained its greatest beauty.

The "Lombardic" capitals shown in figure 29 present a useful and interesting style that is less formal in character than the Roman. Those shown on page 58 have been selected with a view to their occasional use for reproduction by process.

*If the craftsman will study carefully the various forms of the same letter, and then try to reproduce the spirit of them in one of his own, he is more likely to produce capitals that will combine well than if he simply copies existing forms.

Wherever Latin was in use, the Roman form of writing was employed as a matter of course, whether written by an Italian, a Gaul, a Spaniard, or a Briton, and remained a Roman script. With the advance of independent paths of civilization, the hands assumed grad-

FIG. 29   'LOMBARDIC' CAPITALS BY F.W.G.

ually distinctive characteristics and took on in each country the complexion of its surroundings and varying conditions, developing the national hands. The hand we call "Lombardic" was a develop-

FIG. 30   'CAXTON' INITIALS. [F. W. G. FOR A. T. F. CO.]

ment by the Italians of the old Roman cursive—more especially its development in the South, although the title is applied generally to all the writing of Italy in the Middle Ages, where it prevailed from the eighth to the eleventh century, and is a further transition of the square capitals and rounder pen forms.

Types based on the Lombardic capitals, which at their best preserve much of the feeling of the uncials of the sixth and seventh centuries, seldom retain the freedom of the painted letter and are usually too stiff and formal in appearance to grace the page on which they are displayed.

Lombardic forms are capable of beautiful treatment; that they may be treated freely is an obvious convenience, but may prove, also, not a real advantage. Taste & judgment are imperative for their best use. The earlier forms were simple and beautiful pen shapes, but after the fourteenth century they were often fattened vulgarly and overburdened with ornament, losing many of their essential char-

FIG. 31   SPANISH CAPITALS, FROM ARISTOTLE'S ETHICS. [CIRCA 1458]

acteristics. As painted, they take on an appearance somewhat different from that of the pen-drawn forms. [See page 58.]

Visigothic, or the national hand of Spain, is similar to the Lombardic and became an established text in the eighth century, persisting until the twelfth. At first extremely crude & illegible, it later became fine and handsome. A characteristic of the text was a tendency to extreme elongation of the limbs of the letters.

Merovingian, the national hand of France, was made up largely of loops and angles in a cramped irregular way. Its derivation is the same as that of the Visigothic, & though the writing of the seventh century is practically illegible, that of the eighth may be read almost easily. One characteristic of the hand, as in the Visigothic, was an elongation of the up and down strokes, which occurred even in the capitals. This hand and the preceding one present little of value as patterns for the student-craftsman.

Celtic, the national hand of Ireland, was founded on the semiuncial Roman and developed from manuscripts taken into Ireland by missionaries. It is bold, clear, & frequently of great beauty, lending itself to some of the most wonderful achievements of penmanship in the history of calligraphy; but although it is of intense interest to the student, it does not present much material for the present-day artist in his everyday work.

"Types to they that be of the Craft are as things that be Alive, & he is an ill Worker that handleth them not gently and with Reverence. In them is the power of thought contained, and all that cometh therefrom."

A TYPOGRAPHIC SOLECISM

This type face has been designed by Fred W. Goudy for his own amusement. For his lower-case letters he has drawn on the half-uncials of the fourth, fifth, sixth, and seventh centuries, eighth-century uncials, suggestions from the types of Victor Hammer, Rudolf Koch, and others; with these he has attempted to combine majuscules based on square capitals of the fourth century, rustic hands of the scribes, to which he has added his own conceits. If the face has any quality of interest it is due to Mr. Goudy's audacity in bringing the various elements that compose it together in one font. Of course an uncial required no majuscule, since it was in itself a sort of majuscule; therein, he thinks, lies the Solecism.

The matter above is set with the ordinary characters of the font; for matter of an archaic nature, special characters shown in this paragraph have been provided.

Goudy "Mediaeval" shown here is a new type based on a 12th-century South German MS. which, if judged by pragmatic standards, may not meet the approval of critics who demand in types the elimination of any atavistic tendencies.

FIG. 32   24-PT. 'TORY,' AT TOP; 12-PT. 'FRIAR,' CENTER;
AND 24-PT. 'MEDIAEVAL,' AT BOTTOM

CHAPTER VII : The Development of Gothic

THE FOUR varieties of writings which finally merged into the one we now call "Gothic" are variations upon the Roman capital. The Gothic form is a characteristic one. By the thirteenth century it had become a distinct style, and within the next hundred years it reached its highest perfection, although some individual scribes clung tenaciously to the older forms, which were round & free and easier to write. The later, more regular and straight-backed letter was revived by the early printer after it had gone out of fashion for a time, as he found it simpler to imitate in type.* It was the use of the reed pen by the medieval scribe in writing the Roman letter that gave it its Gothic character. The quill pen which the Italians employed held the ink better & was more pliant than the reed, making the minuscule letter rounder and with greater variety in the thick and thin strokes; it came into general use with the use of paper.

This leads to the statement that the character of all lettering is directly due to the tool employed. The stylus merely scratched the surface of the clay or wax, and gave us the cuneiform character; the chisel gave us the clear-cut classic inscriptions in stone; the reed pen, blunt strokes with thick ink on papyrus; the quill, the round full-bodied form.

In the stone-cut capital the cutter felt the need of a neat square cut to end the stem of his letter. To define the free end, a sharp cut

*Not the form of the letter itself; as written, the letters ran together and interlocked in a way too difficult to accomplish with separate type bodies, except by the use of a great many "tied" characters [two or more letters on one type body].

[66] was made across it with the chisel, and as the chisel was usually wider than the thin line, this cut extended beyond it on each side. Probably for the sake of uniformity, corresponding extensions were added to the thick strokes, & what was at first merely an attempt on the part of the craftsman toward neat workmanship later became an essential part of the letter itself. These endings are called "serifs" or "cornua." With the pen the serif definitely finished the

gothic minuscule

FIG. 33   MEDIEVAL GOTHIC MINUSCULES

free endings & added to the squareness and finish of the letter, but as the fluid ink was inclined to drag and bracket at the junction of the stem on the side toward the direction of the stroke, the scribe deliberately added to the opposite side to make both uniform in shape. Serifs preserve and accentuate the regularity of the line of lettering.

With the pen the pressure is not naturally in the middle of the stroke, but at one end. In forming the letter 'O,' instead of the symmetrical Roman form the Gothic 'O' is the more natural one. It was easy to cut the Roman form in stone & preserve symmetry. Gothic letters are essentially written forms made with one stroke of the slanted pen, and while the Caroline letters written in the same way kept an open, round appearance, in the Gothic, for the sake of greater economy of space, the curves were reduced to straight lines [at first of scarcely varying thickness], making the letters narrower, more angular, and stiffer, until the written page was made up of rows of perpendicular thick strokes connected at the top & bottom by oblique hairlines. Gothic capitals, however, tend to roundness, and in a way are incongruous; but they do break the monotony of an exceptionally rigid form of minuscule, perhaps happily, although they seldom seem to belong to them. The glory of the Roman alphabet lies in its capitals, while that of the Gothic letter lies in its lower case. This is but natural, since the Roman alphabet originally was

NO. 1   NO. 2   NO. 3   NO. 4   NO. 5   NO. 6

FIG. 34   VARIATIONS OF GOTHIC CAPITAL 'A'

an alphabet of capitals only. In Italy alone the earlier roundness was preserved, & while of course affected later by the Gothic tendency, the letters never entirely acquired the extreme angularity of northern European writings. The fifteenth-century formal writing of the Italians became the foundation of the roman types which now supersede all other forms for printing books.

Figure 34 shows six variations of the Gothic 'A' drawn by craftsmen of different nationalities at different periods: No. 1 is from the tomb of Richard II, about A.D. 1400; No. 2, from an English chancery manuscript of the fifteenth century; No. 3, from the work of Albrecht Dürer, early sixteenth century; No. 4, from an Italian manuscript of the sixteenth century; No. 5, from a seventeenth-century Flemish Gothic type form; & No. 6, from an alphabet dated 1901, by the American architect, Bertram G. Goodhue, well known for his achievements in the Gothic style.

ABCDEF
GHIJKLM
LNOPQ
RSTUW
VXYZ&

FIG. 35 'GOUDY TEXT' CAPITALS, DRAWING FOR TYPE

Late Gothic is narrow and condensed in the extreme, the letters have angular & acute corners, and the ascenders and descenders are shortened with marked loss of legibility. [See fig. 33.] When a form was evolved in which the amount of black overbalanced the white, it

abcdefghijkln
mopqrstuvxy
wz1234567890

FIG. 36 'GOUDY TEXT' LOWER CASE, DRAWING FOR TYPE

was called "black-letter." As in all pen-drawn forms, the broad lines are the down right-sloped strokes; but as the intrinsic value of Gothic lies in its freedom, no absolute rule for the form can be stated. Gothic quality applies rather to the spirit than to exact form, as every individual letter may have several quasi-authoritative shapes, each of which is acceptable if it preserves an intelligent conception of the spirit of freedom, which is the essential of Gothic lettering.

[70]   The large word "Alphabet" on the title page of this book, drawn by the writer, is based on the Gothic lettering shown in the plates [pp. 105 ff.] and illustrates the slight changes necessary to give an entirely fresh aspect to traditional forms. The lower-case letters are variations of the Italian round hand.

"Tory Text," by F.W.G. [see fig. 32, p. 64], is based on the sixteenth-century "lettres bâtardes" of Geofroy Tory of Bourges as shown in his book, 'Champ Fleury,' on the correct proportions of letters—"the most useless and most curious work on lettering in existence." I have made many departures in my translations of Tory's letters into type, simplifying the forms and redrawing a number to meet the requirements of legibility for modern eyes.

"Goudy Text" is a freely rendered Gothic letter, composed from various sources. This sort of letter, being less perfect in form than the roman character, lends itself to a greater variety in design. Originally written with single strokes of a slanted pen, it kept a round, open appearance, which later gave way, for greater economy in space, to more angular, stiffer, and narrower forms, until finally the written page consisted, in large part, of rows of perpendicular thick strokes connected at top and bottom by oblique hairlines. The types of Gutenberg and his associates, as well as those of his immediate successors, were founded on the Gothic medieval minuscule of Germany, a hand that stood apart from the writings of other countries; indeed, it never attained the beauty of other national hands. In Italy the traditional roundness was preserved, and although it never acquired entirely the angularity of its northern neighbors, it was nevertheless somewhat affected by the "Gothic" tendency.

Gothic lettering became a distinct style in the twelfth century; [71]
but the term "Gothic" when applied to a style which belongs not to
one, but to all the Germanic tribes, is a misnomer. In fact, the title
did not come into existence until centuries after any people called
Goths had passed from the earth. Moreover, "Gothic" was at first a

PACK MY
BOX WITH

FIG. 37   DRAWING FOR 'LINING GOTHIC' TYPE BY F.W.G. [1924]

mere random expression of contempt, a title of depreciation & scorn.
Everything not of the classical Italian forms the critics dismissed as
"Gothic," meaning rude and barbarous thereby.

Printers' Gothic is a rude imitation of classic Greek and Roman
lapidary capitals. Its lack of grace & its unpleasing monotony when
used in a succession of lines make it unsatisfactory except for a single word or a line where greater blackness is desired than is possible
with the usual roman forms. Its use is occasional, and some real demand for a letter of this character should be clearly evident, since it
possesses very little grace or beauty. It must be spaced carefully if
awkward gaps between irregular letters are to be avoided. It is im-
properly named "Gothic." In England it is more accurately called
"sans-serif," and in Germany it is named "Grotesk."

CHAPTER VIII : The Beginnings of Types

TYPES constitute the simple & inevitable corollary of the written books that preceded them. Written forms of letters were shaped for easy reading, the scribes simplifying and dropping everything difficult for the pen to shape easily. Types based on those pen forms were simplified still more because of technical and mechanical limitations, but not at the expense of beauty, as printing came at a time when the illuminated manuscript had reached its greatest period of perfection, and fifteen centuries of artistic traditions furnished beautiful models for the printers' use.

Printing began as an aid to the art of the scribes, not as an independent art, and at first was used mainly, if not entirely, to supplement their work. In this connection "printing" does not here mean pages of text printed from movable types, but the use of engraved blocks, many bearing engraved legends, which were printed before the descriptive text was written in. Examples of such manuscript books with printed illustrations are to be found in the British Museum and in Continental libraries. The illustrations were printed because the skill of the copyists was unequal to so great a task and, although it was expedient to engrave the pictures, it was as yet inexpedient to engrave the whole text. This was at the beginning of the fifteenth century. With the invention of movable types the situation took on a new aspect & the work of the copyist fell into disuse, while that of the illuminator or decorator of books correspondingly increased in importance; but the invention of printing was the death blow to the beautiful book letters of the scribes.

At the time of the invention of printing from movable types, two styles of writing were in general use, & so there naturally came into being two styles of type faces, roman and black-letter. For nearly a century after the invention, black-letter was the preferred form, not only in Germany, but also in Holland, England, France, and Spain,

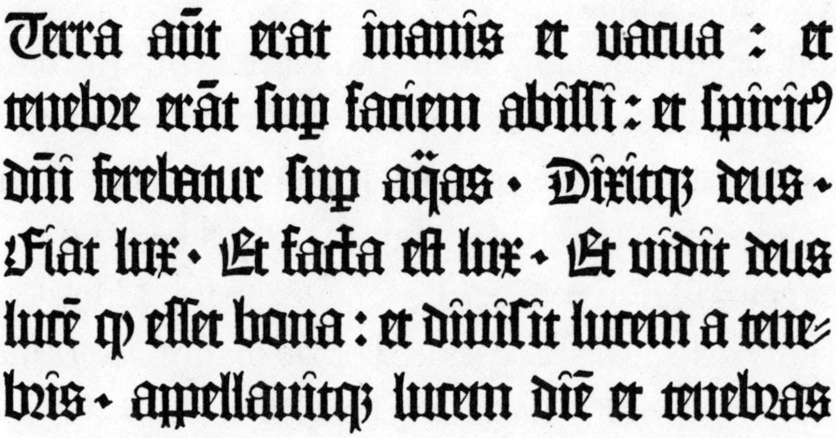

Terra aūt erat inanis et vacua: et tenebre erāt sup faciem abissi: et spirit͞ dn͞i ferebatur sup aq͞as · Dixitq; deus · Fiat lux · Et facta est lux · Et vidit deus luce͞ q eslet bona: et diuisit lucem a tene͞ bris · appellauitq; lucem die͞ et tenebras

FIG. 38   TYPES CUT FOR THE NATIONAL PRINTING OFFICE AT PARIS
FROM THE TYPES OF THE BAMBERG BIBLE OF 36 LINES

although as early as the year 1464 roman type letters of a crude form appeared in Germany, nearly as early as at Rome. Why the hostility to the simpler roman forms was so widespread we cannot understand, for the roman alphabet certainly required no defense after more than fourteen centuries of use in the preservation of literature. One reason for the general use of black-letter was that its heavy face and lack of fine lines made it easier to cast, and in printing it would not show signs of wear so readily as the roman form. The greater compactness and boldness of the black text to which the ordinary book buyer had been familiar all his life is probably what impelled Nicolas Jenson, designer of the most nearly perfect letter, to print in Gothic text in order to make his books more salable in northern

[74] Europe; just as Ulrich Gering in Paris was obliged to discontinue printing in roman letter and revert to black. In order not to prove huddled and ineffective, light-face roman types were of large size, open & round of form, with abundant white space within each letter as well as between lines. Large types meant large books and additional cost in the making.

The first attempt at economy in production was the reducing of white space between lines & words, and the neglect to paragraph; next, the reduction in sizes of types. Jenson, Ratdolt, & Renner had put black-letter on small bodies, but there had been no attempt to crowd the round-faced roman into smaller space. Aldus found that his beautiful books in large types and broad margins were unsalable. To get buyers he must make smaller and cheaper books and make smaller types for them.

Type shaped itself, we might say, accidentally. At first, it was based on manuscript forms, probably with the intention of deceiving readers into the idea that the printed books were manuscript; whether that was the intention or not, it was the only way to make books readable to eyes accustomed only to manuscript pages. In a short time it became apparent that the considerations which controlled the scribe no longer concerned the printer. He discovered that one shape was as easy to print as another, & this discovery brought about an attempt at a revision of the alphabet in the direction of greater legibility. At first, thought was given to beauty of form as well, but later attempts to bring letters into a given space by compression or reduction to meet the exigencies of printing did not necessarily satisfy the true ends of art.

The styles of the early types were not invented by the punch cutter; usually he was directed by the printer to imitate the letters of
some preferred manuscript as closely as he could.

We of today have been reared on print, with all its mechanical
smoothness and precision. We have little, if any, ideal of lettering,
and little feeling for the charm of character and individuality that
only hand work gives. No one can look at an early printed book without feeling the beauty of the type page, for the old printers' types
were inspired by the letters of the handwritten books, & with these
for models they played endless variations on the alphabet, while our
present types in the main are absolutely monotonous, with no artistic flavor or thoughtfulness.

The first types were Gothic, & the earliest specimen of printing
to bear an authentic date is the Letter of Indulgence issued by Pope
Nicholas V to the King of Cyprus in his war with the Turks, printed
at Mainz in 1454, and now preserved at The Hague. It consists of a
single sheet of vellum, measuring 11 by 7 inches, & is printed on one
side only. Some of it is in the same type as that used in the Mazarin
Bible, and as it was issued from the press at Mainz, it is reasonable to
imagine it was printed by Gutenberg. The first book to bear a printed
date is the Schoeffer Codex of 1457.

I am assuming that Johann Gutenberg of Strassburg was the in-
ventor of movable types, and that John Fust, a goldsmith and rich
burgher of Mainz, assisted him with money, the two jointly printing
the Mazarin Bible. It is conjectured that the metal types used by the
early printers were cut by goldsmiths, & hence it is easy to conclude
that Fust's skill as well as his money contributed to Gutenberg's

[76] service. Their type was modeled on the familiar manuscript hand of the time. The Bible bears no date, but in the copy of it preserved in Paris the rubricator's inscription shows that it was completed before August 15th, 1456. The type is known to have been in existence in 1454, and it is not likely that it was cut before 1450, the date Gutenberg entered into partnership with Fust.

Printing did not spread rapidly for many years after its birth. In 1462 there was one shop at Mainz under Fust & Schoeffer, and possibly Gutenberg was still working there, too; Pfister was at Bamberg, Mentelin & Eggestein were at Strassburg; these four were all. After the sack of Mainz, Ulrich Zel established a press at Cologne, and gradually printing spread throughout Europe.

We come now to the first radical improvement in the printing art, the beginning of the roman type character, in 1465. It was then that Sweynheim & Pannartz began printing in the monastery of Subiaco near Rome. Theirs was the first press established in Italy, and the first book printed in that country was Cicero's De Oratore. The type used was neither black-letter nor roman, but a type that was black-letter in color but nearly roman in form.

Their type shows plainly an unconscious leaning of its designer toward the mannerisms of the Gothic black-letter, the only form of letter used until these printers established their press. This transitional type, then, marks the beginning of the roman type form; it is the prototype from which all other roman types are descended, and for that reason is extremely interesting, & furthermore, it presents a valuable pattern for radical departure. Exactly as the designer of this type used the Gothic letter with which he was familiar and cre-

ated a new form, so should we, in creating our new forms, make use
of the letters of the great periods as a source of inspiration.

In the same year, 1465, that Sweynheim & Pannartz were printing in their transitional type at Rome, another printer at Strassburg
was using a distinctly roman letter, as was Gunther Zainer at Augs-
burg in the following year; and in 1470, at Paris, Ulrich Gering & his

Here ends The Treatyse of Fysshynge wyth
an Angle, set in type by St John Hornby and
Meysey Turton & printed by the first-named
at the Ashendene Press, Shelley House, Chel-
sea in the year 1903 after the text of the Boke
of St Albans 'enprynted at Westmestre by
Wynkyn the Worde the yere of thyncarnacion

FIG. 39   ASHENDENE PRESS TYPE, BASED ON THE
TYPE OF SWEYNHEIM & PANNARTZ

associates printed from the first roman types in France. The types
of these early printers, while unlike those of Sweynheim and Pannartz, were all simple and legible, and not without beauty; but the
real development of the roman letter had its beginnings in Venice.
John of Spire & his brother, followed by Nicolas Jenson, began printing there in 1469. "Jenson," William Morris said, "carried the roman
type as far as it can go." This type, which has been the inspiration
for all fine roman types since 1470, is the first roman type form of distinction; round & bold, it has great beauty, and the individual forms
are in perfect symmetry and accord in combination. [A lower-case
letter is shown on each full-page plate.] Jenson had an instinctive
sense of exact harmony in types, and he was so intent on legibility
that he disregarded conformity to any standard—an innovation that

[78] modern designers might well consider. Jenson's original inspiration was, no doubt, some fine manuscript book; but, realizing the essential difference between the written character, where every repetition of a letter had naturally some subtle quality of difference & variety, and print, where each repeated letter was an exact facsimile, he conceived his types as forms cut in metal and considered his model forms only as suggestions. He brought to this work his experience as master of one of the French mints, where he engraved coins. It is said that in 1458, at which time rumors of the new art of printing had reached France, Charles VII sent him to Mainz to learn the secret and bring it back to France. He did return to France in 1461, but, meeting with a cool reception from the son of Charles, who had not his father's interest in such matters, he did not long remain there, and turned instead to Italy, whither the printing tide flowed. Here his activity was great & the fame of his work spread beyond Venice, so that Pope Sixtus IV called him to Rome and conferred upon him the title of Count Palatine. Even within his lifetime his types were acclaimed as the true Venetian characters, as "sublime reproductions of letters."

It would seem that the wonderful type of Jenson, the designs of Ratdolt, and the excellent work of contemporary printers should be glory enough for one city, but the fame of Venetian typography is further enriched by the great Aldus Manutius, first for his celebrated editions of the Greek classics and later for that slanting character which he called "Chancery," but which was named "Aldine" by the Italians in honor of the maker. In France, where this new form was counterfeited, it was called "italic," the name by which it is still known to French and English readers, while in Germany & Holland, where it was almost at once copied, it is called "Cursiv." In a decree dated November 14th, 1502, the senate of Venice gave Aldus the exclusive right to his character; but although his patent was renewed by Pope Alexander in 1513, he had no real protection, as the man who cut his type for him from the handwriting of Petrarch made duplicate punches for a rival printer, who reprinted Aldus' edition of Vergil, not only stealing the new form of letter, but his editorial work as well. Other printers made imitations, & one at Lyons, known as "the Honest Man Bartholomew Trot," reproduced the Vergil and other Aldine classics in close imitation, even with the trade-mark of Aldus, and sold them as productions of Aldus' press.

From this time on, printing sank lower & lower—French or Low Country printing remaining neat but without distinction. Worst of all was the English, and it was not until about 1724, when William Caslon cut the fine fount of type now known as "Caslon Old Face," that any revival of early excellence was realized. Before Caslon's type was cut, it is said there was more Dutch type in use in England than there was English, & his letter is probably based on an Elzevir model. His type is clear and neat, well designed, and, as originally cut, full of variety and life; but as recut [and it has been imitated by all the type foundries] it has lost everything of feeling and vitality, retaining the form only. As Caslon cut each character painstakingly on the end of a steel punch, with few instruments of precision, judging form and proportion solely by eye, his type shows variations in the forms and proportions of the same letters in different type sizes, and shows those natural irregularities in execution which are always the indication of a mind intent on design and personal expression.

[80] Toward the end of the eighteenth century, Giambattista Bodoni, an Italian printing at Parma, exercised a very great influence on the types of his contemporaries. While his types are absolutely devoid of any artistic quality, being so regular & precise in line that a monotonous effect is produced, Bodoni and his school furnished the models for type founders until 1844, when the Chiswick Press of London revived Caslon's famous founts. The new vogue of Caslon's "old face"

COMPARATIVELY FEW PEOPLE CARE
anything about Art, and when they do it is because they mistake it for something else.

FIG. 40   18-PT. 'GOUDY MODERN'

influenced other founders to cut new "old style" letters. Bodoni's type displayed in a marked manner an attenuation of the thin lines, with a reduction of the graduated portion of the curves to a minimum. The letters are thereby weakened in construction and turn a page into a maze of heavy lines fretted here and there with grayness, so that the eye is constantly readjusting its focus. Morris says of it that it is the most illegible type ever cut, with its preposterous thicks and thins; he even speaks of "the sweltering hideousness of the Bodoni letter." Newdigate, the English writer, says the ugly modern face which we owe to Bodoni is still used almost exclusively for certain classes of work. Most of the text pages of our magazines and newspapers are set in a modern face. The type shown in figure 40 is the result of an attempt to produce a type face which will redeem "the ugly modern face we owe to Bodoni" from the charge of illegibility under which it now rests.

CHAPTER IX : The Qualities of Lettering

IN PREPARING this manual the author has endeavored, as far as possible, to present the subject in the order that appeared to him most helpful to the student of lettering, and it may seem to some that he has given undue space to the beginnings of types & printing. His reason is that as practically all the drawn lettering employed today is to be printed as type or in combination with types, & as the lettering should be in exact harmony with those types, no better models for drawn letters can be found than fine types based on the letters of the handwritten books.

Before the year 1500, letters were chiefly pen forms & were pen-produced, but though they did influence the shape of the forms we now employ, it is no longer necessary, except in the occasional formal written book, to carry the qualities inherent in pen forms into letters produced by other methods and for other purposes.

It is to be understood in all that follows regarding lettering that formal writing is not meant, but instead, lettering intended for book covers, title pages, advertisements, types, etc., and such lettering is properly 'drawn,' not 'written.' One writer has gone so far as to maintain that drawn letters are wrong and written ones only are right. He does admit that the Roman capitals of the Trajan inscription are not entirely pen forms. If there is one exception, why not others? There is no doubt that the capitals of the Trajan Column were first painted in before cutting, but that is hardly writing. In formal writing, where the actual work of the artist is seen and read, neither reproduced nor duplicated by mechanical process, the lines should be formed with-

[82] out sketching, retouching, or correcting. Each letter should be simple [having no unnecessary parts], distinctive, and legible, and should show, too, the use of the pen. But if the work is to be reproduced by a mechanical process in which any corrections or retouchings will not be discoverable, there can be no good reason for omitting or neglecting such corrections if greater clearness or better appearance is gained.

The author does not feel that formal writing should be reproduced by process at all; it is in the actual forming of the letters that the personality of the craftsman is strongly expressed, and this personal quality is practically lost when the work is duplicated by process, which takes no account of the varying degrees of color, etc., and the reproduction presents only a flat & lifeless copy. In this handbook, formal writing*is touched upon as a matter of historical interest only.

Collections of alphabets removed from their original habitats, early stone-cut inscriptions, manuscript books, etc., do not always present adaptable forms upon which to found an individual style. Such letters while entirely suitable for use for some specific place or purpose might mislead the beginner, until he has learned something of the history and development of letters, into mistaking mannerisms of the scribe for the essentials of structure. For this reason, the pattern alphabets presented here are, for the most part, type forms, since they are the natural and inevitable materialized letters of the scribes, that is, handwriting divested of the scribes' vagaries and whimsicalities, conceived as forms cut in metal, simplified and for-

*Formal writing is adequately dealt with in the volume, *Writing, Illumination and Lettering*, by Edward Johnston. Macmillan & Co., New York.

malized to meet new requirements and new conditions of use. They
are simple shapes to be modified & given new expressions of beauty just as they themselves were adapted and simplified from the forms of far-off times. And since nearly all lettering is intended to be used as type or in connection with types, hand lettering enters to an appreciable degree within the limitations imposed by type.

Lettering based on or suggested by accepted type forms does not deny the artist ample opportunity to shape his letters more freely or space them more precisely than fixed and implacable metal types allow, since he may, by some slight adjustment or modification of the shapes of his model letters, persuade his forms to accommodate themselves to each other in a manner almost impossible with ready-made types. The use of these type models as a foundation tends also to keep the craftsman's rendition of them clear of any excrescences, meaningless lines, or additions not necessary to their fundamental or essential elements; neither will their use as patterns in any way preclude the thought of beauty to be attained by the perfectly legitimate variations that good taste & common sense may dictate.

Well selected and carefully drawn type forms, copied without radical changes of shapes, will often be found to appeal to the artistic sense and add to the decorative value of the page where used, to a degree not always attained by prim types, since the artist's handling of line will give variety, a quality of life, and a freedom seldom found in types ready to one's hand.

Yet slavish copying of the examples given is not recommended [except so far as is necessary to familiarize oneself with their structure]; they are patterns to be studied, that the principles of form and

[84] construction underlying each specimen may be discovered. Each one drawn ought to convey one clear idea, and one idea only—what letter it is—so that the eye need not stop to disentangle the essential form from any eccentricities of handling, nor be drawn to the conceit of a craftsman intent on a display of his own skill at the expense of the work he is expected to embellish. It is the personal quality he injects into his work, not freakish variations or unnecessary additions to his pattern letters, that will determine its character.

There may be times when the decorative quality of a line of lettering is of greater value than easy legibility, but this fact should not be made an excuse to deform letters for the sake of expediency, nor to produce any unusual shape without exceptional artistic warrant.

Letters are not to be measured, nor is there any canon of proportion to set up. Broadly speaking, they must be either Italian [roman] or Gothic. It does not matter whether they are based on the circle or on the square—whether "old style" or "modern," the essentials are the same; the chief difference lies in the matter of proportion. One word, however, on the use of Gothic, today little used as a text letter: for lines in which the decorative quality is of greater importance than easy legibility, this style presents an opportunity for compactness and color impossible in the roman forms.

Pleasing legibility is the foremost consideration. One offense to avoid is extreme attenuation of any lines, as this involves constant alteration of the focus of the eyes, which, though slight in the reading of a few words or a line, is extremely wearing in the aggregate. Ruskin struck the right note when he advised the craftsman not to make lettering illegible when the only merit present is in its sense, by attempting beauty at the expense of use. He directs: "Write the Commandments on the church wall where they can be plainly seen, but do not put a dash and tail to every letter." Where the eye can rest is the place for decoration. The idea that a page is made beautiful only at the expense of legibility is a vagary of artists who lack knowledge of the art with which they meddle.

In the first place, simplicity of form is necessary; this requires a study of the essential root forms, which are practically those of the lapidary capitals of two thousand years ago. Each of those characters had an individuality. By emphasizing this characteristic quality in such a way that nothing in it inclines us to confound any letter with its neighbor, we may get a new expression or quality of personality, which is as far as we may go, since those forms are now fixed. A craftsman possessing individuality will express himself in his work and endow it with character, with that personal singularity which is the quality that gives distinction to any work. There should be no attempt to make designs of individual letters, since design implies invention, and what already exists cannot be invented.

Some alphabets are in themselves in the highest degree so decorative that there is danger in using them except for a word or two, as the repetition of the elements contributing to their decorative quality is bound to be irritating. In the manuscript page every repetition of a character took on a subtle quality of difference; in print every repeated letter is in facsimile. The artist should, then, study his model until he has grasped the spirit of it, selecting characteristic forms and simplifying them for his use, to avoid any element of restlessness.

[86]   In the construction of a letter the artist must decide first what is its intrinsic shape, that is, in what degree are the lines, curves, and angles, or the directions the lines take, that compose it, fixed. His next thought should be for form, & on his decision here will largely rest the measure of his ability. If the form is fundamentally wrong, no added ornament by way of disguise will rectify it. Its character must be organic, and more often than not a form developed simply

J. VASQUES, FIRST TO PRINT IN THE CITY OF TOLEDO, MCCCCLXXXVI

FIG. 41   'HADRIANO' TYPE BY F.W.G., BASED ON STONE-CUT LETTERS
OF THE FIRST CENTURY

without conscious effort toward beauty but with due recognition of its essential quality will result in real beauty.

The ancient craftsmen who cut the historic inscriptions in stone were more concerned for a consistency in the proportion of their letters than with mere details of execution; their work was not a matter of conscious or elaborate design. Apart from the proportion of the forms, the character of the stone-cut letter is that given by the tool used in its making, but the form itself is that produced by brush or pen. This is natural, since the letters were probably painted in before the cutting was done.

"Hadriano" type [an example of which is shown in fig. 41] was designed by the author, who reversed the process, and from a rubbing of a few letters from an inscription of the first or second cen-

tury produced a type conceived in the same spirit as the original cutting, a design unique in the annals of type founding.

Study the accepted model until the essential form can be reproduced without conscious effort; but do not forget that a letter or
style that is good in one material and suited to a definite purpose

FIG. 42   SIX VARIATIONS OF   LOMBARDIC 'A'

cannot always be adapted [even by brute force] to another material,
place, or purpose, although the underlying principle of its structure
may be used as a basis for a new rendering. Many letter forms are
indeed interchangeable; but if it is desired to adapt lettering of one
class to the purposes of another, certain differences of treatment are
inevitable to make them suitable to the medium employed. Thought
based on knowledge, good taste developed by analysis of beautiful
forms, and modesty, will go far toward attainment of style.

Figure 42 presents six drawings of a Lombardic capital 'A', freely
rendered from a sixteenth-century service book, to illustrate a point
the author desires to impress on the beginner—that he is free, if it
seems advisable, to copy any letter shown in this book; but copying

[88] is not the best way to develop his individuality. Rather let him get at the underlying form and cautiously work out his own variations. These six drawings show the slight changes necessary to give each letter a different aspect without destroying its harmonious quality or losing the generic likeness. [For another example see the capital 'A' in the word "Alphabet" on the title page of this book.]

| UNCIAL 7TH CENTURY | ENGLISH 8TH CENTURY | CAROLINE 9TH CENTURY | ENGLISH 10TH CENTURY | ENGLISH 11TH CENTURY | ITALIAN 12TH CENTURY | ITALIAN 16TH CENTURY | F.W.G. 20TH CENTURY |

FIG. 43   DEVELOPMENT OF LOWER-CASE 'g' FROM THE ROMAN UNCIAL

The main reason for the use of drawn lettering is that it is more easily addressed to the artistic sense than are set and fixed type forms, & that it becomes, itself, the decoration of the page. Beautiful letters, as such, are out of place for the text of books, where easy reading is the chief desideratum and where symmetry is of less importance. For the decoration of the page, however, the type ready to one's hand does not always serve. Qualities of greater account than mechanical precision or regularity are needed, making the drawn character necessary; but no license is thereby permitted to the artist to take undue liberties with the proportions of letters. True, the crossbar of an 'A' or 'H' may be shifted up or down within limits, and so on, but that is not what is meant. It is one thing to disregard tradition, but quite another to go beyond the bounds of moderation. In lettering itself there is not much scope for originality, but there are so many varieties of letters from which to choose that the artist may devote all his arts of design to their arrangement and expression without finding it necessary to invent mock forms.

The test which a well-formed letter must meet is, that nothing in it shall present the appearance of being an afterthought—that every detail shall at least seem to have been foreseen from the start; and, when letters are used in combinations to form words and sentences, that no one of them shall stand out from its fellows or draw attention to itself at the expense of those with which it is associated.

CHAPTER X : Some Practical Considerations

IN THE construction of a letter the artist should first determine just what the intrinsic shape of his model is—that is, in what degree are the lines, curves, & angles, or the directions the lines take that compose it, fixed or absolutely necessary to that particular letter. His next thought must be for form, which includes proportion and beauty, and the particular form suitable to the place & purpose for which it is intended. His decision here will largely determine the measure of his ability and taste. A letter should possess an esthetic quality that is organic, an essential of the form itself and not the result of mere additions to its fundamental form nor to meaningless variations of it.

These points, also, must be kept clearly in mind: First, what is the purpose of the lettering, whether for a title page, a book cover, a line or more for an advertisement, a poster in which probably it must harmonize with a picture [neither overriding nor in turn being robbed of its own value]. Second, what is the right letter to use for a given purpose, not only suitable to that purpose, but also practicable for execution in the material employed. A letter drawn with a broad pen and suitable enough on smooth paper might be entirely out of place if cut in brass and stamped in gold or color on the cloth covering of a book. Third, the selection of letters that will combine well with each other and with the matter with which they are to be used. Some letters, such as "Lombardic" [fig. 25, p. 58], used generally as initials or as capitals with the Gothic lower case, and entirely pleasing when so used, are yet ordinarily quite incompatible for the formation of words. Even in roman alphabets the power of combination may be lost by careless handling; certain letters coming next to others of the same family may require slight modifications to bring them into harmony with those of less sympathetic form in order that the eye may be carried easily to their neighbors. Fourth, the relative size of the letters. This point may require experiment to determine the limits of variety permissible without sacrificing beauty or effectiveness of arrangement.

Pleasing legibility is the great desideratum. Beauty, too, is desirable, but beauty must not be emphasized if it detracts from easy readability. Beauty is an inherent characteristic of simplicity, dignity, harmony, proportion, strength—qualities always found in an easily legible type; yet legibility is seldom achieved by a predetermined effort to produce it. To attempt consciously to give a specific character or beauty to a letter is too frequently, also, to exhibit the intellectual process by which it is sought; its character seems to have been thought in & does not appear to be the outcome of a subtle and indefinable taste that makes it delightful & seemingly the obvious and inevitable thing.

The beauty of a letter depends on the harmonious adaptation of each of its parts to every other in a well-proportioned manner, so that their exhibition as a whole shall satisfy our esthetic sense—a result gained only by blending together the fine strokes, stems, and swells in their proper relations.

Above all, it should be accepted that in lettering there is very little scope for originality in form, since the fundamental shapes of letters are now fixed; nor should the artist attempt to design letters, since

[92] design implies invention, and that which already exists cannot be invented. Mere copies involve loss of vitality—every real work of art, even the humblest, is inimitable.

The architect is bound by the laws of structure; the artist and craftsman are bound, too, by laws more mental than physical, yet none the less real or binding. While certain fundamental forms seem to demand certain sequences, the excellence of the final product de-

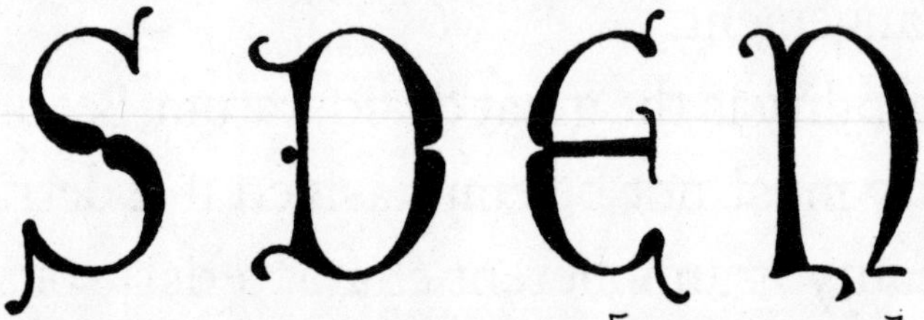

SDEN

FIG. 44   LOMBARDIC PEN FORMS. [13TH CENTURY]

pends entirely on the fertility of the artist's mind. As in other forms of design, the workman in drawing letters should use the technical limitations of the craft in which he works, to its own advantage. He should not endeavor by trickery to obtain results in one material or method that by right belong to others. Nor should he undertake to master that which in the nature of things is not to be overcome. He should endeavor to express all that belongs to his particular work, yet not attempt also that which can be expressed properly only by other and quite different means: he should not draw in line to imitate the technique of a woodcut, design a type that is to give the effect of a letter engraved on copper, or draw letters that are to be reproduced by process to simulate a manuscript book hand, etc. The very limitations imposed upon a craftsman free from whims, who understands fully the necessity for directness, will add beauty to all good work produced by him within those limitations.

Chapter XI : Notes on the Plates

Each plate shows fifteen forms of one letter of the alphabet, each corresponding form occupying a similar location on every plate, so that a note regarding a form of letter shown in figure 45 on this page will refer to any letter shown in the same position on each of the large plates. Each plate includes a historical note on the letter shown, which the craftsman may find of interest though of no great aid in making variations from the forms given.

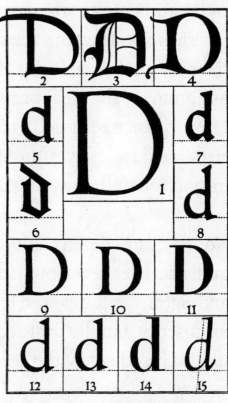

FIG. 45   KEY TO PLATES

No. 1   A letter from the inscription on the base of the Trajan Column at Rome, cut A.D. 114. The stone on which the inscription appears is, within the molding, 3 feet 9 inches high by 9 feet ¾ inch long, with lettering in six lines almost filling the free space. The letters in the two upper lines are each about 4½ inches high, those in the next two lines 4⅜ inches, in the fifth line 4⅛ inches, and in the last line 3⅞ inches. The serifs are small and carefully formed, the thin or hair lines about half the thickness of the thick stems. The curves of B, P, and R should be noted. The characters H, J, K, U, W, Y, Z are not present, but forms such as might have been cut are shown in their appropriate places. With the utmost care to retain all the subtleties

[93]

[94] of form & proportion, these capitals have been drawn by the writer from a photograph of the inscription purchased by him at the British Museum. No finer capitals on which to base new expressions are to be had, and they may be accepted as the root forms of western European lettering.

The "Forum" capitals shown in figure 11, page 38, were designed by the author in an attempt to render the spirit of the classic lapidary inscriptions. They are the first types ever cast "distinguished by their successful rendering of classic feeling. . . . The capitals known as Forum are the most beautiful and have been widely used & imitated." [BRUCE ROGERS.] "Forum" capitals retain the spirit of the ancient lapidary letter, although comparison with those of the Trajan inscription will show differences in the forms of individual letters.

No. 2   Slanted pen capital, originally produced by reed or broad quill pen, later developing into the straight pen uncial of the seventh and eighth centuries. The letters shown are not from any particular manuscript, but illustrate the form naturally produced by the scribe using a broad pen with the square capital as a model.

No. 3   Gothic or black-letter capital, the gradual outgrowth of the round Roman uncial shown in figure 18, page 51. This form, which has persisted & is still in use as an ornamental letter, is descended from the fifteenth-century writing of northern Europe. It is one of the most picturesque forms, and very ornamental, although individual letters may seem illegible. The letter shown is a free rendition of a type form from the Caslon Foundry, called "Caslon's Old Black."

No. 4   Lombardic Gothic versal. Manuscript versal forms [so called because used to denote the beginnings of verses, paragraphs, etc.] were built-up Roman letters which in the tenth & twelfth centuries departed from the more severe Roman form by the addition of ornamental features, or by curving and fattening the strokes. They developed or degenerated into the Lombardic—not invented by the Lombards, or even confined to northern Italy, but first developed in Lombardy and hence so called. These capitals are used mainly as initials & often are not written, but painted in, which accounts somewhat for the fatter strokes. See figures 26, page 59, and 28, page 60.

No. 5   Italian round-hand minuscule—from the writing book by Vespasiano, 1556. It varies but little from the manuscript hands of the fourteenth century. It is based on the old Roman uncial [see fig. 18, p. 51] and retains some of its peculiarities, preserving its roundness. This letter form never acquired the extreme angularity of the Gothic, and became the foundation of our roman small letters or lower-case forms, which have superseded all others. With this letter, Gothic capitals, either black-letter or Lombardic, are used. Note the word "Alphabet" on the title page, also figure 24, page 57, showing type of Ratdolt, both being variations of the Italian round hand.

No. 6   Gothic or black-letter minuscule, the type form used for the first printing by Gutenberg & Fust—taken from a facsimile of the type of the Bible of 36 lines [fig. 38, p. 73]. The medieval minuscule of Germany stands apart & never attained the beauty of either the northern or the southern hand; nevertheless it furnished the model

[96] for the first types. In Italy a more refined taste went back to an earlier time in search of a more beautiful standard of writing, which was brought to perfection soon after the middle of the fifteenth century, just at the right moment to be adopted by early Italian printers.

No. 7   The second type of Sweynheim and Pannartz, in which the compression, blackness, & modified angularity are a little less pronounced than in their first type [shown fairly reproduced in fig. 39, p. 77], which showed a marked leaning toward Gothic mannerisms. Theirs was the first attempt to cut the roman form of letter in type and marks the transition from Gothic to roman, although it is neither Gothic nor entirely roman, but Gothic in color and nearly roman in form. It is the prototype of our roman lower-case letters and therefore of great interest, & a form on which the designer might well exercise his artistic attempts at letter design. These letters have been drawn freely from facsimile reproductions, my intention being solely to preserve the general effect, the actual details of serifs, etc., having been lost in bad presswork and inadequate reproductions.

No. 8   Type of Nicolas Jenson, the first pure roman type face, and of great distinction & beauty, not so much in the design of the individual characters, which are round and bold, as in the perfect harmony and symmetry of the letters combined in a page. No one character dominates, each takes its proper place; the letters hang together and show at a glance the great difference between the round open roman form and the somber angular black-letter. It was on this form that William Morris based his "Golden" type. The craftsman can find no better roman letter on which to form a style. These drawings are from photographic enlargements of the types used by Jenson in printing his Eusebius.

In the type shown in figure 46, the writer believes that he has re-discovered the principle of spacing individual types in use by Jenson & his contemporaries, but not since—a principle to which the harmonious quality of a page of Jenson is largely due. Every letter stands

QUOD NICOLAUM IPSUM EX
urbe roma istuc salvum adventasse
scribis gratulor, et eo magis quod et com⁄

FIG. 46 'GOUDY LANSTON,' ILLUSTRATING
JENSON'S PRINCIPLE OF SPACING TYPES

on solid serifs of unusual shape, so planned as to make each letter form coterminous with its type body while maintaining enough white space to set each letter off from its neighbor & preserve to the greatest degree the unity of the word formed by the separate characters. This permits close spacing of words and avoids loose composition. A type page full of white gaps is not clearly framed by its margins, nor is it in pleasing harmony with them.

Nos. 9 & 12   "Kennerley" type, designed by the author. So named because first used in a volume published by Mitchell Kennerley [first publisher of 'The Alphabet']. Of the "Kennerley" an English writer says: "This type is not in any sense a copy of early letter—it is original; but Mr. Goudy has studied type design to such good purpose that he has been able to restore to the roman alphabet much of that lost humanistic character which the first Italian printers inherited

[98] from their predecessors, the scribes of the early Renaissance. Besides being beautiful in detail, his type is beautiful in the mass. . . . Since Caslon first began casting type in 1724, no such excellent letter has been put within reach of English printers."

Nos. 10 & 13   "Caslon Old Face," designed and cut by Wm. Caslon in 1724, and the first type of any distinction to be used in England.

LIFE WITHOUT INDUSTRY IS GUILT,
life without Art is brutality.

FIG. 47   24-PT. 'GOUDY OPEN,' A MODERN TYPE FACE

This letter presents the perfection of unassuming craftsmanship, & lacks any artistic pretensions; it is straightforward, legible, with a quality of quaintness and even beauty that secures for it general favor. It is perhaps better known by name to all who use types than any other face; but few realize that the face today bearing the name differs greatly from the original cutting by Caslon. Comparison of the same letters in different sizes of Caslon's types shows considerable variation. The writer has used what he considers typical forms, regardless of the different type sizes from which they were taken.

Nos. 11 & 14   Types of Bodoni, the Italian printer, cut about 1771. He made his hairlines thinner and the stems thicker than had been done in any previous cutting of roman types, & cut his letters with a sharpness & regularity never before equaled. He considered his designs as having been executed with a broad pen, but with a broader pen than anyone else had ever attempted to use. The copperplate

quality of his types gave his print a sharpness and brilliancy that is $\quad$
somewhat dazzling [not clearly indicated here, owing to the large
size of the letter].

The type shown in figure 47 is the result of an attempt by the author to design a modern-face letter with a quality of interest and legibility not present in the types of Bodoni and his school.

✓ ✓ ✓

No. 15 "Kennerley Italic," designed by the author to accompany the
roman face shown in Nos. 9 & 12. The inclined dotted line shows

ACTA PAGANA RESURGUNT

FIG. 48 24-PT. 'KENNERLEY ITALIC' CAPITALS

the slight degree of slope, probably as little inclination as that of
any italic known, the italic quality of the forms not making greater
inclination necessary. The capitals are shown above [fig. 48].

In 1497 Aldus described his printing in his new italic letter said
to be copied from the handwriting of Petrarch as "like writing by
hand, but with a hand of metal."

✓ ✓ ✓

The last plate shows four renderings of the ampersand or 'short
and,' a character which is practically a monogram of the letters 'E'
and 'T,' or the Latin 'et,' that is, 'and.' The notes preceding regarding
Nos. 2, 3, and 8 apply to these. No. 1 is the Caslon italic form. The
figures given directly under and on each side of '&' are from an old
brass [A.D. 1520], and the lower set is a free rendering of Caslon's
old-style figures. Arabic figures were introduced into Spain A.D. 950,
into France in 991, and into England in 1253.

[100]   As a matter of graphic convenience the letters 'v' and 'u' began to vary, until in the tenth century the 'v' form was by preference used as the initial and 'u' as the medial letter. Similarly, in the fifteenth century, 'I' was lengthened & turned to the left at the beginning of words as a sort of ornamental initial, and, as the consonantal sound usually occurred at the beginning and the vocalic in the middle of words, the two initial forms of 'V' and 'J' became specialized to denote consonants, and the medial forms 'u' and 'i' to represent the vowels. The form 'U' is of recent introduction, as the early printers used a 'U' with two thick vertical strokes, to which our lower-case form is similar.

The dot over the 'i' was introduced in the fifth or sixth century A.D., although at first it was merely an accent to indicate double 'i,' the single 'i' being written without any accent.

The preceding chapters present no royal road to lettering. The student must do his own work, draw his own conclusions, & rediscover for himself the fundamentals which the writer has attempted to outline. When the craftsman has mastered the essentials, he may then devote all his efforts to new departures.

Mechanical affectation of finish will not in any degree take the place of real knowledge of forms; imitations of early craftsmen's work will not necessarily produce results fit to present needs. Study shows that their productions were strictly within the bounds of severe conventions, influenced by the environments & conditions under which they worked. To make our work meet present requirements and satisfy human needs, the craftsman must now, as then, enter sympathetically into the details and incidents of the lives of [101] the users of his work, and recognize fully their necessities and obvious habits; therefore work produced under other and different conditions will seldom present more than a basis for new expressions.

In using the older patterns we may depart radically from the suggested forms, or even engraft upon them a character derived from other sources or styles, if always we can persuade them into something fit, harmonious, consistent, and satisfactory. Nor should we forget that the best work includes a degree of beauty aside from its strict utilitarian purpose, as beauty in any useful thing supplies a very real demand of the mind and eye.

To present properly & fully a history of the development of each of the roman forms we use would require many more words than the limited space under the Trajan capitals on the plates following will permit. The meager notes given are mere outlines and intended only to present those facts which can be given in a few words, & should be read in connection with each other and not independently, as the evolution of many letter forms is dependent upon that of others.

THE PLATES

A corresponds to the first symbol in the Phoenician alphabet, where it represented not a vowel, but a breathing, the vowels not being represented at all. This breathing not being necessary in the Greek language, the Greeks, who adopted the Phoenician alphabet, used it to represent a vowel.

B corresponds to the second symbol of the Phoenician alphabet, and is the second letter in all
European alphabets except those derived from
medieval Greek [i.e., Russian, etc.].

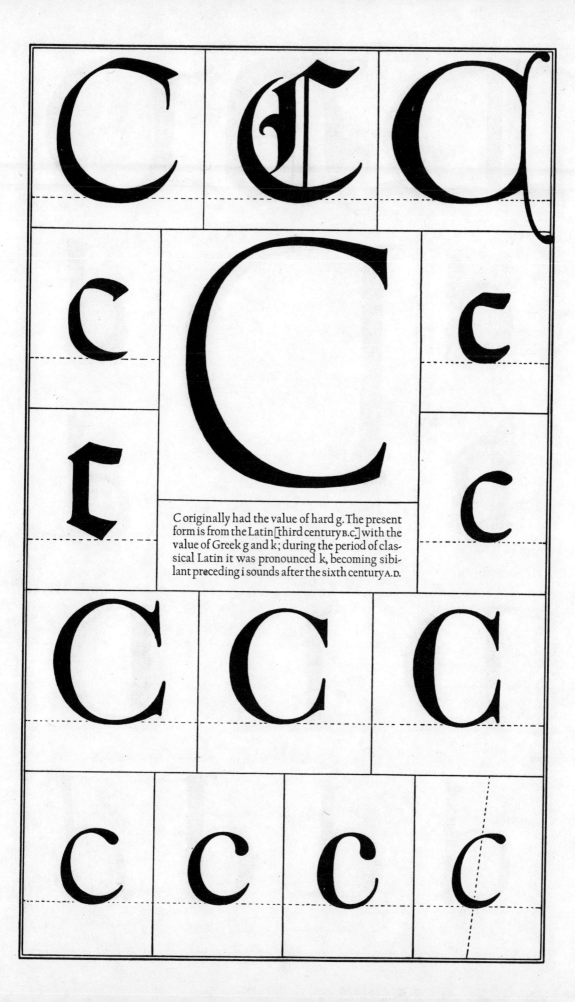

C originally had the value of hard g. The present form is from the Latin [third century B.C.] with the value of Greek g and k; during the period of classical Latin it was pronounced k, becoming sibilant preceding i sounds after the sixth century A.D.

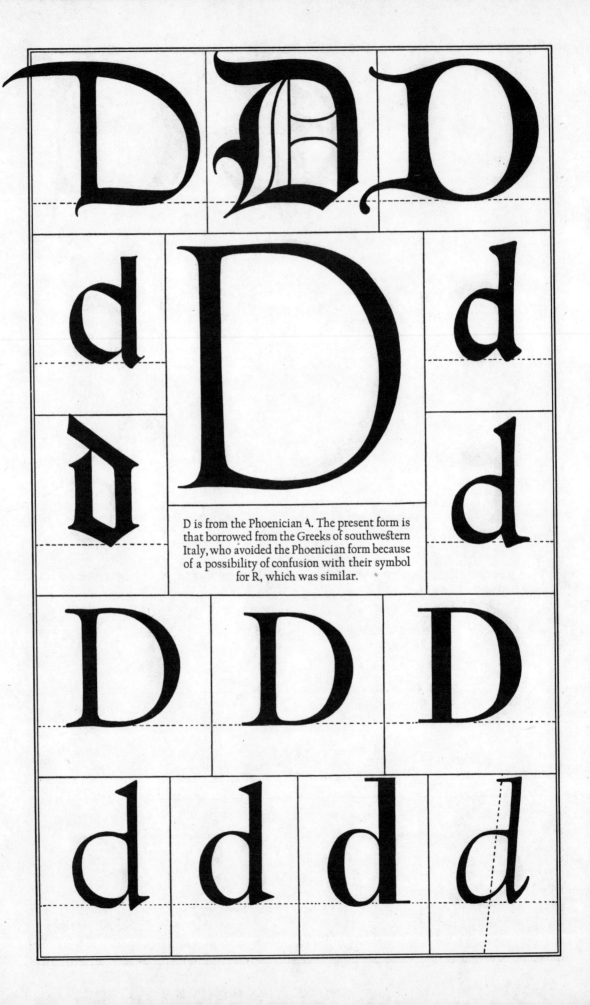

D is from the Phoenician Δ. The present form is that borrowed from the Greeks of southwestern Italy, who avoided the Phoenician form because of a possibility of confusion with their symbol for R, which was similar.

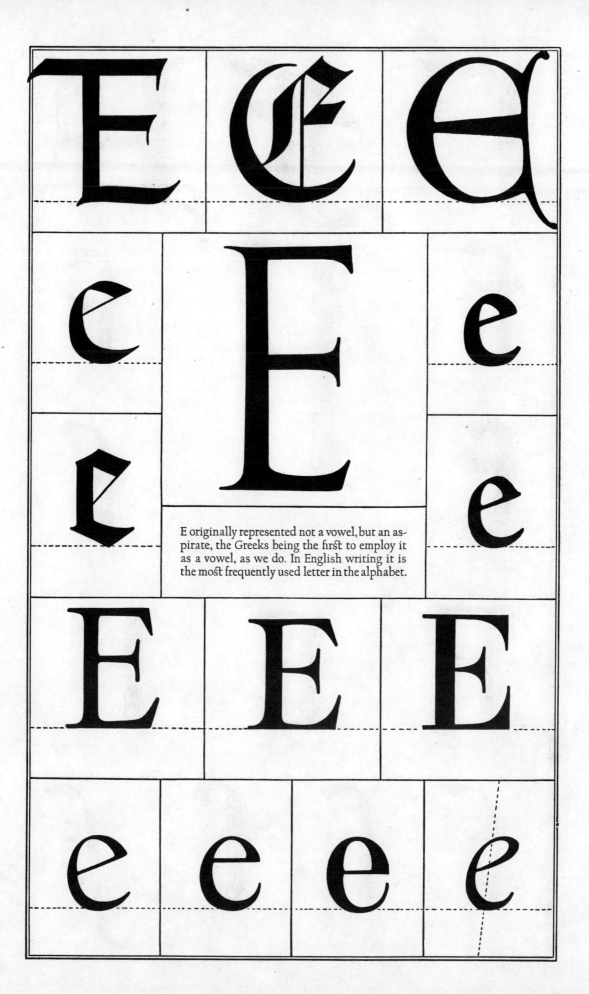

E originally represented not a vowel, but an aspirate, the Greeks being the first to employ it as a vowel, as we do. In English writing it is the most frequently used letter in the alphabet.

F is from the early Greek ⌐, which had the value of w. The Greeks had no sound corresponding to the Latin f. The Romans, who adopted the Greek letters with the Greek values, used F to represent the sound of ph.

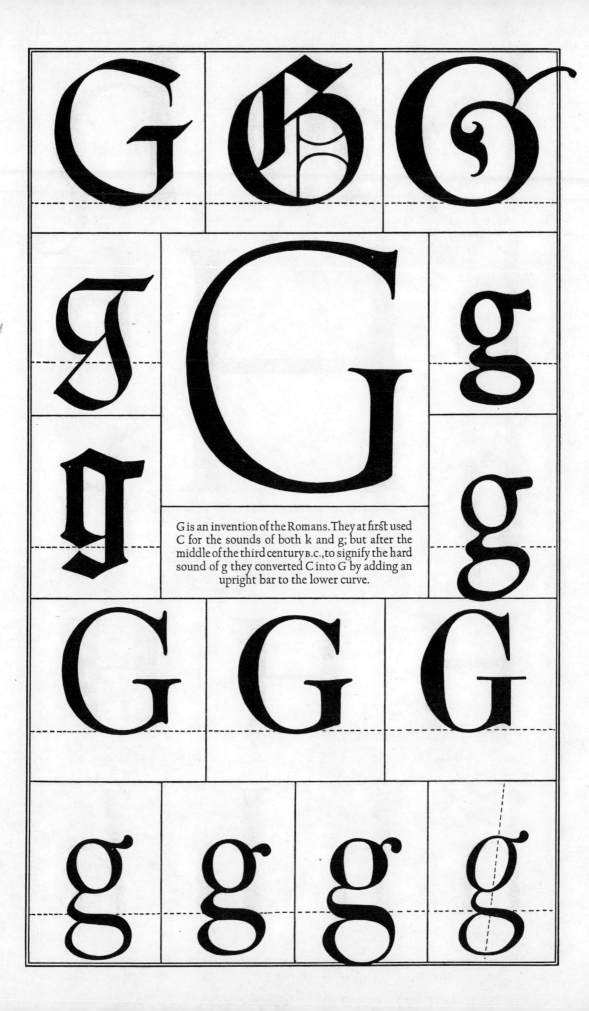

G is an invention of the Romans. They at first used C for the sounds of both k and g; but after the middle of the third century B.C., to signify the hard sound of g they converted C into G by adding an upright bar to the lower curve.

H, as an aspirate, was borrowed from the Phoenicians by the Asiatic Greeks; but they, soon losing
the aspirate, used it to represent the long e-sound.
The western Greeks retained the aspirate longer,
and the Romans, who adopted their alphabet, used
H as an aspirate only, as we do now.

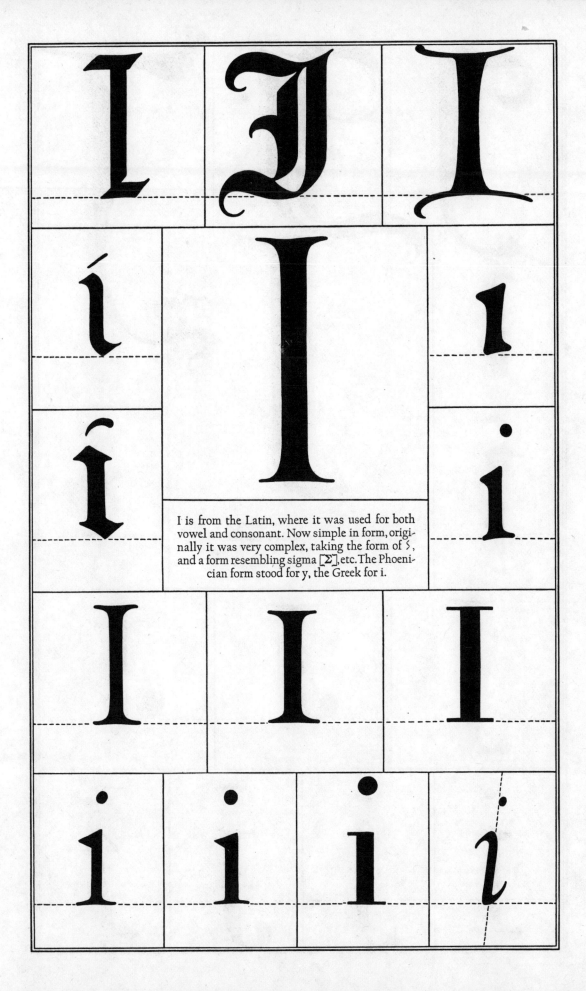

I is from the Latin, where it was used for both vowel and consonant. Now simple in form, originally it was very complex, taking the form of ſ, and a form resembling sigma [Σ], etc. The Phoenician form stood for y, the Greek for i.

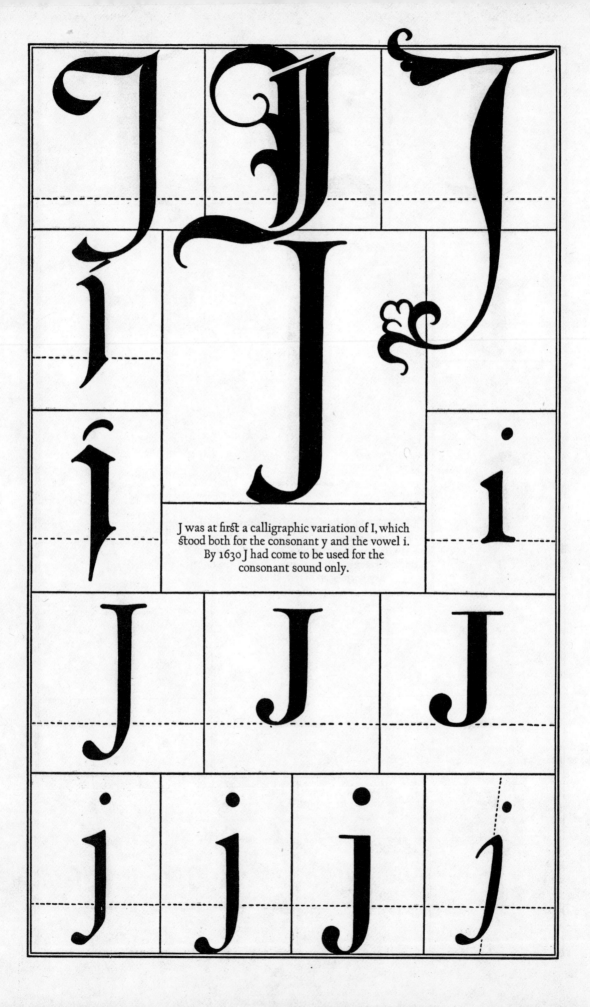

J was at first a calligraphic variation of I, which stood both for the consonant y and the vowel i. By 1630 J had come to be used for the consonant sound only.

K has changed very little, first appearing on the Mo-abite Stone [early ninth century B.C.], but written from right to left, ꓘ, and probably changing to the present form when the Greeks transposed the Se-mitic mode of writing. It was sometimes written K.

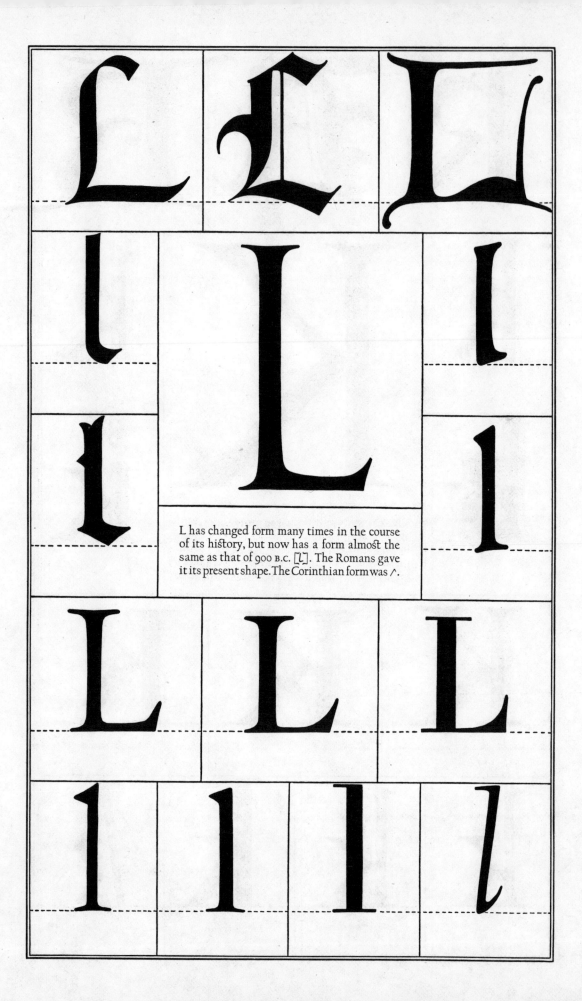

L has changed form many times in the course of its history, but now has a form almost the same as that of 900 B.C. [L]. The Romans gave it its present shape. The Corinthian form was ʌ.

M as we make it is a late Roman form, the early
Greek mu with legs of equal length representing not m, but s. The oldest Latin inscriptions
show M with a fifth stroke, ⋀⋀.

N in its earliest form had its first limb longer than the others, but the Greek and Latin tended to make all of equal length. The inscription on the Trajan Column shows no serif at the joining of the first and the diagonal strokes.

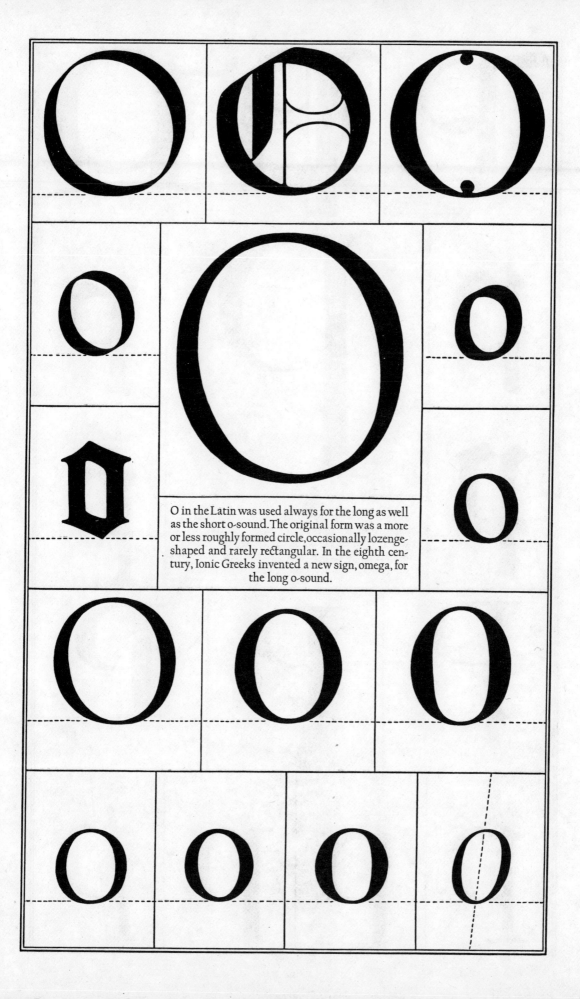

O in the Latin was used always for the long as well as the short o-sound. The original form was a more or less roughly formed circle, occasionally lozenge-shaped and rarely rectangular. In the eighth century, Ionic Greeks invented a new sign, omega, for the long o-sound.

P in its earliest form was Greek in shape, Γ, later becoming rounded in the Roman; in Imperial times the semicircle was completed, giving the present form, although early Roman inscriptions show the lower curve not joined to the stroke, P.

Q is never used alone [except as an abbreviation
and sometimes in transliterations of Hebrew to
denote a more guttural k], but is always combined
with U, with the sound of cw, which QU replaced
to avoid the ambiguity of C.

R in the Phoenician, written somewhat like the symbol for D, became, in early Greek, ᛣ, the tail being introduced later [although not a universal practice] to avoid confusion with D.

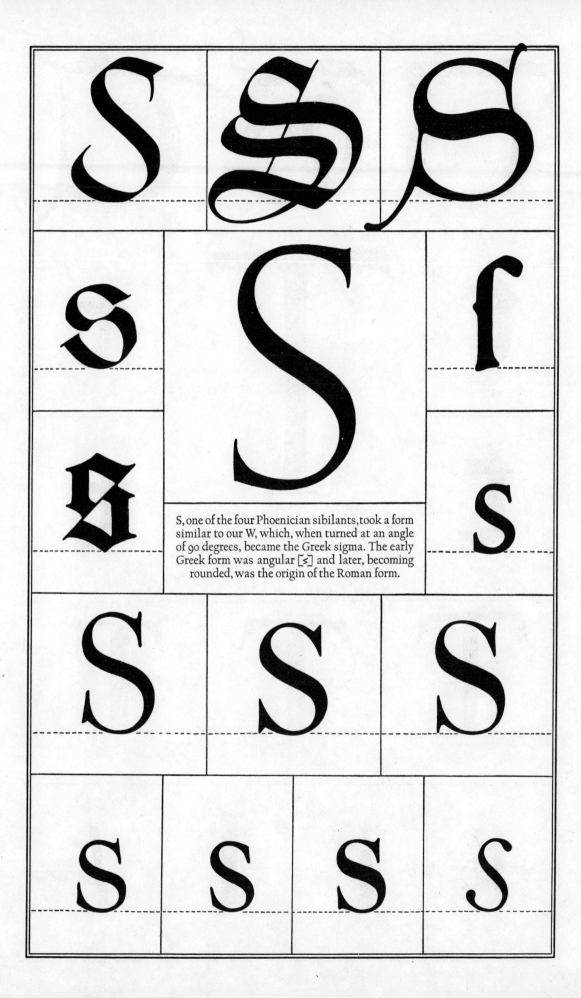

S, one of the four Phoenician sibilants, took a form similar to our W, which, when turned at an angle of 90 degrees, became the Greek sigma. The early Greek form was angular [ϟ] and later, becoming rounded, was the origin of the Roman form.

T in its Phoenician form was that of a St. Andrew's cross, ✕, which is the form shown on the Moabite Stone. The Greek and Latin forms were practically those of the T we use.

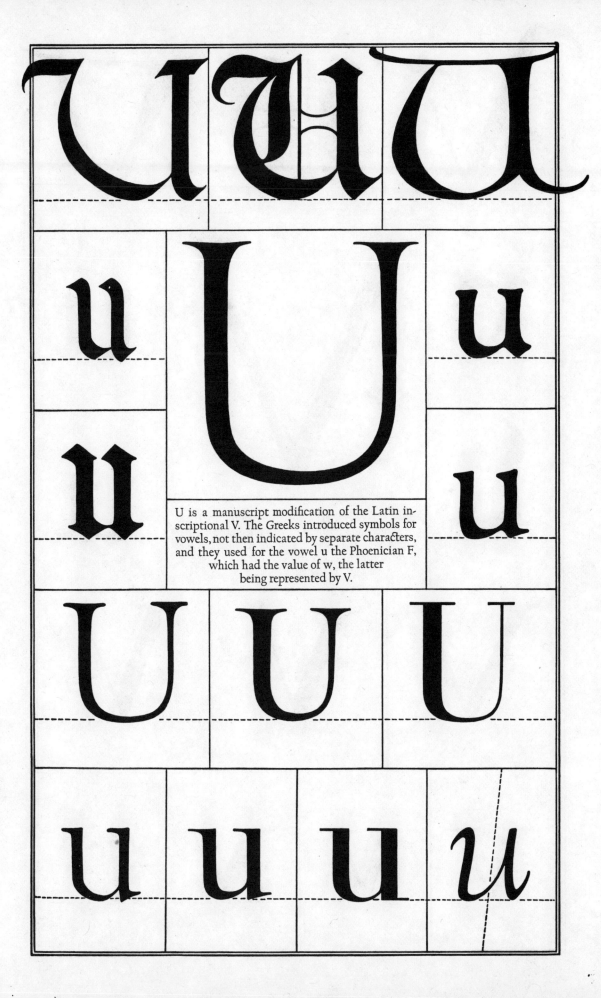

U is a manuscript modification of the Latin inscriptional V. The Greeks introduced symbols for vowels, not then indicated by separate characters, and they used for the vowel u the Phoenician F, which had the value of w, the latter being represented by V.

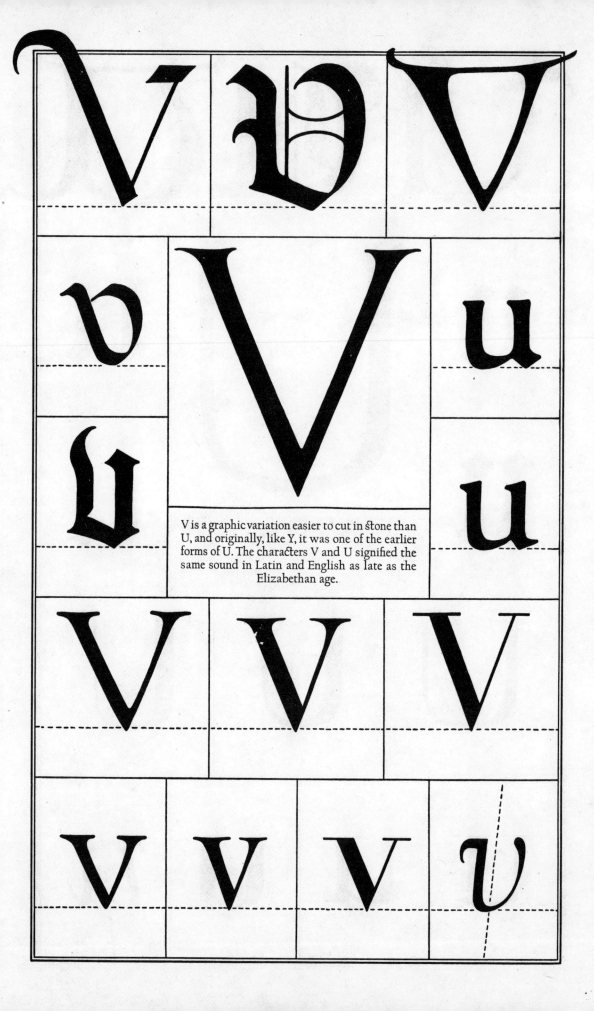

V is a graphic variation easier to cut in stone than U, and originally, like Y, it was one of the earlier forms of U. The characters V and U signified the same sound in Latin and English as late as the Elizabethan age.

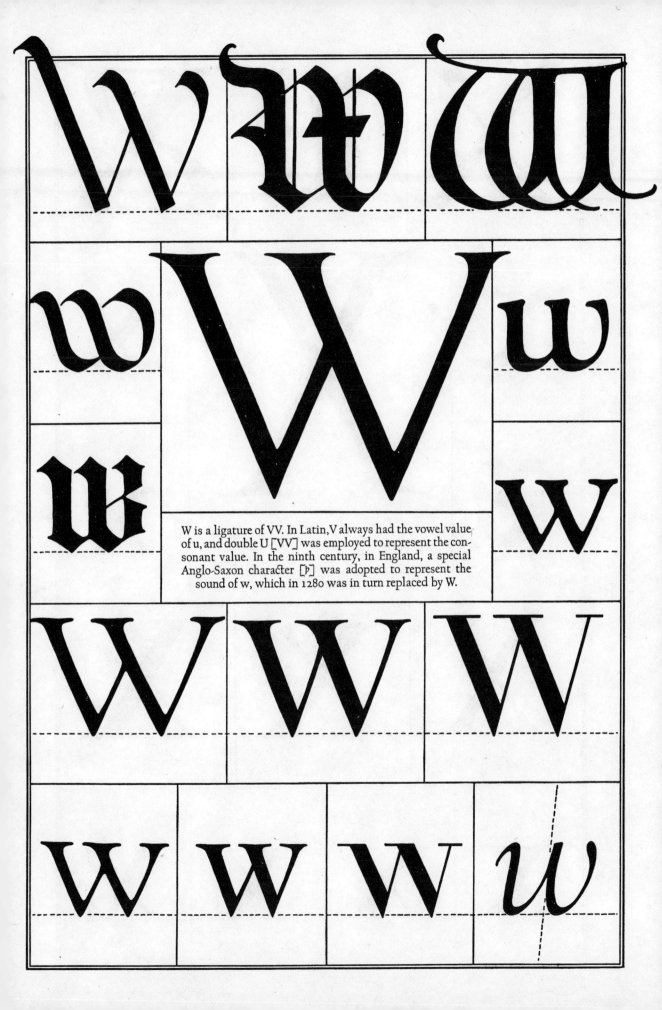

W is a ligature of VV. In Latin, V always had the vowel value of u, and double U [VV] was employed to represent the consonant value. In the ninth century, in England, a special Anglo-Saxon character [Þ] was adopted to represent the sound of w, which in 1280 was in turn replaced by W.

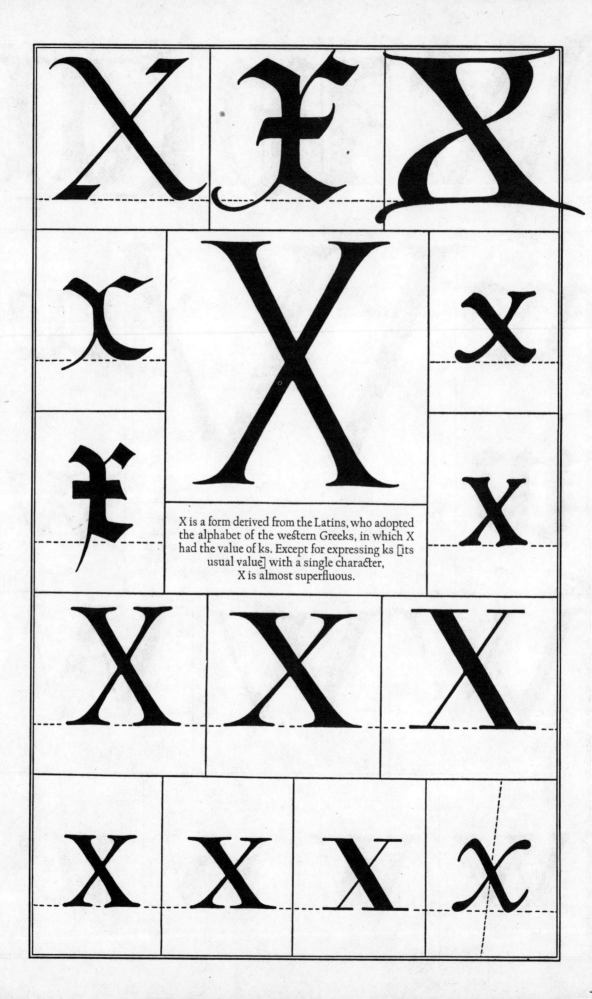

X is a form derived from the Latins, who adopted the alphabet of the western Greeks, in which X had the value of ks. Except for expressing ks [its usual value] with a single character, X is almost superfluous.

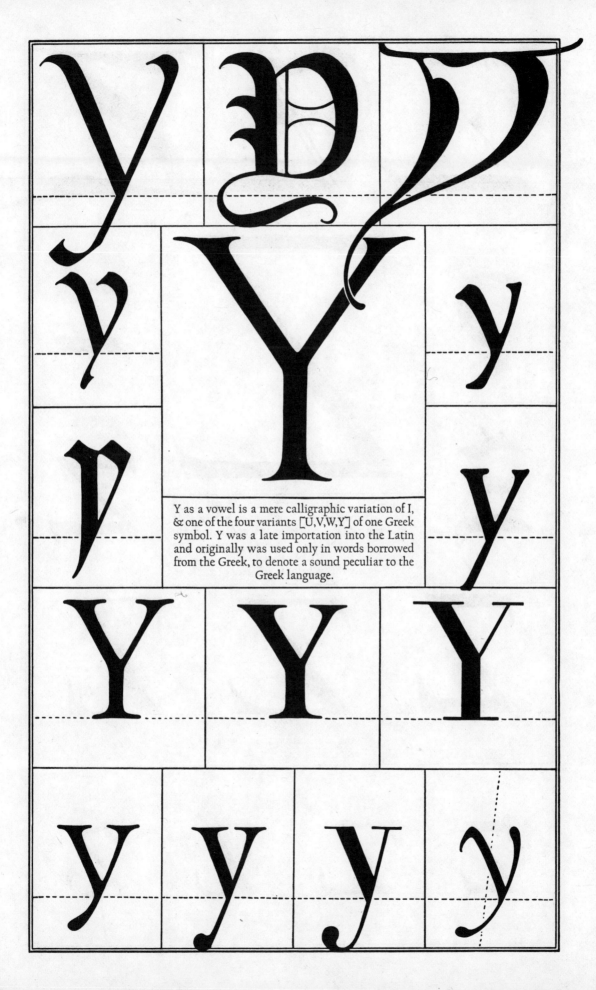

Y as a vowel is a mere calligraphic variation of I, & one of the four variants [U,V,W,Y] of one Greek symbol. Y was a late importation into the Latin and originally was used only in words borrowed from the Greek, to denote a sound peculiar to the Greek language.

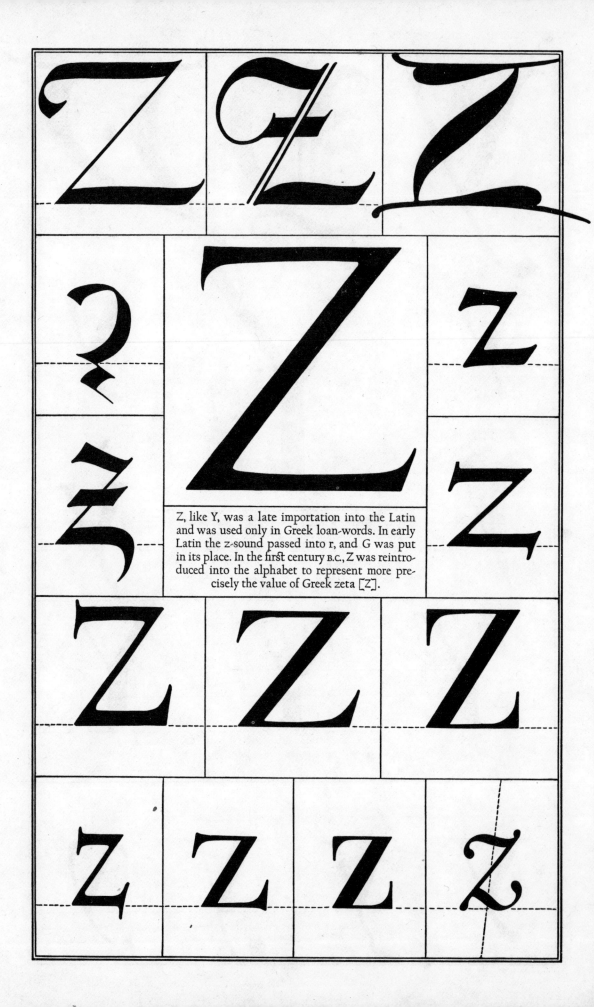

Z, like Y, was a late importation into the Latin and was used only in Greek loan-words. In early Latin the z-sound passed into r, and G was put in its place. In the first century B.C., Z was reintroduced into the alphabet to represent more precisely the value of Greek zeta [Z].

  & & &

1 & 3

2   4

5 6 7 8 9 0

1 2 3 4 5

6 7 8 9 0